Children's Stories by
Grandma Dee Dee

Delores (Dee) Ray

Copyright © 2022 by Delores (Dee) Ray.

ISBN 978-1-64133-790-8 (softcover)
ISBN 978-1-64133-721-2 (ebook)

All rights reserved. No part of this book may be reproduced or transmitted in any form or by any means, electronic or mechanical, including photocopying, recording, or by any information storage and retrieval system without express written permission from the author, except in the case of brief quotations embodied in critical reviews and certain other noncommercial uses permitted by copyright law.

This book is a work of fiction. Names, characters, places, and incidents are the product of the author's imagination or are used fictitiously. Any resemblance to actual locales, events, or persons, living or dead, is purely coincidental.

Printed in the United States of America.

Brilliant Books Literary
137 Forest Park Lane Thomasville
North Carolina 27360 USA

Contents

A Story about My Mom 5
A Trip to the Farm 7
Christmas Story by Grandma Dee Dee 15
Amanda and Her Friend 20
The White Fawn 24
Christmas Cookies 30
Christmas with Grandma and Grandpa 34
My Friend the Grasshopper 38
Dressing Up 41
Halloween 43
The Poor Little Church Mice 57
Going to Fairyland 66
The Pink Cloud 77
Timmy 80
God Gives Me Opportunities 83
Sarge 87
The Green Frog 91
The Magic Gown 95
Thunder: Megan's Friend 99
Grandmother's Remedy 103

The ABC Story 107
The Sad Dog 111
The Mouse's Tea Party 119
A Trip To The Cabin 122

A Story about My Mom

I have to tell you that I have the most special mom in the world! I'm only 3 years old, and my mother's name is Maureen. From the time I was very little, she took care of me because my dad and mom weren't married. She always looks after me and makes me happy.

I worry about her because she has to go to work early in the morning and take me to the babysitter's. Bundling me up in warm clothes, she hauls me off when I'm still half asleep. Sometimes I'm very crabby, and I don't like to be awakened so early in the morning.

She dresses me in my snowsuit in the middle of winter. We have hats, and we have gloves. We have overshoes. She puts all of those things on me before she takes me to my babysitter and goes off to work.

She always picks me up at night, takes me home, and feeds me. After dinner, she reads me stories.

I just have to worry about her sometimes. I think, *Gee, I have a young, beautiful mother. She works so hard. Someday, everything will turn out fine for her, and she'll have someone to help her.*

I don't know how to tell her, but I think my mother is very special. She has blonde hair and blue eyes. She looks after me very well, takes me to fun things, and is a very good cook. She even reads books to me.

Helping Kids Be Happy

I think I'm very lucky to have such a special mother. The reason I know she is a good mom is because I have gone to several of my friends' houses. Their mothers hardly pay any attention to them, even though their mothers stay home all day. Their mothers seem to ignore them.

Although my mom works very hard, she pays special attention to me and always makes me feel that I am very, very special. She always loves me a lot and gives me a lot of hugs.

I am so lucky to have such a neat mom!

A Trip to the Farm

I like to take a trip to the farm. This happens when Mom gets a message, and, all of a sudden, she says, "Nicole, we're going to the farm." Then we pack a lunch and put it in a large wicker basket.

It's a long way to the farm. We have to drive, drive, and drive. We drive through the city, and then we drive through the countryside.

As we go through the country, we see a lot of green trees and green grass. The beautiful sky is filled with beautiful clouds. We go by the St. Croix River and then come into the little town of Amery, Wisconsin.

Amery is where my great-grandfather lives. We arrive at the farm and get out of the car. There is Grandma! She kisses and hugs us like she hasn't seen us for years. This particular grandmother is Grandma Olson. She has a hunched back and wheezes because she has asthma. In the front yard are rows and rows of beautiful dahlias and zinnias because Grandma likes to garden.

Grandpa has black hair that is about to turn gray. He has a happy face and cheery brown eyes and is very handsome—

much more so than Grandma. Grandma has a different kind of personality. She knits a lot of pretty sweaters for winter and sews all of those nice aprons we wear when cooking.

Hopscotch in the Living Room and Kittens in the Barn

After the hugs and kisses are over, we go into the large white farmhouse. The living room floor has big black and white squares. We hop across it and have so much fun playing on it. Grandma doesn't mind because she doesn't have any carpeting, and she's not the best housekeeper.

In the kitchen, we have milk from the farm. Before we drink it, they put the fresh milk in a big metal separator. It whirls around and separates the cream from the rest of the milk, so we end up with cream and milk. After it's separated, they put it in the refrigerator, and she gives us big glasses of ice-cold milk.

Grandma also has these great big batches of dough for sugar cookies. We help her roll out the dough. This is a great deal of fun. Sugar cookies are the best: large white cookies with sugar sprinkles over them. They're sweet and yummy, and once you start eating them, you want another and another.

Some of our cousins are there. They've arrived just ahead of us. Were all happy to see each other! We decide to go out to the barn because it's late in the evening. This means it's time to milk the cows. They're black and white and are called Holsteins.

This is before milking machines were used, so we go out to the barn and watch Grandpa squeeze all of the cows' milk out of their udders by hand.

It takes several hours to milk this way, as it is all done by hand. After the milking is finished, they separate the milk and bring it into the house to Grandma.

All kinds of kittens live in the barn. They love to have some of the cows' milk. The cats are good hunters and keep the barn free of mice. Some of them are kind of wild, but a couple of the kitties are very tame and let us pet them. They have their own personalities. George Mac, a frisky black-and-white cat, loves to have Grandpa squirt milk from the cow into his mouth. Sally is a soft brown color and is timid until she gets to know you.

Sometimes Grandma lets us bring them into the house for a bit. Kitties are so warm and friendly and make great pets. These kitties do a good job of keeping the barn and cattle feed free of mice.

Strawberry Shortcake and Cock-a-Doodle-Doo

When the barn chores are done, we dash into the house and find that Grandma has made baked chicken for dinner. It's really delicious. It's from homegrown chickens called organic now.

The aroma as we come into the kitchen is heavenly. The chicken is cut up and washed many times. Grandma soaks it in ice-cold water for a few hours. Then she dips it in flour, seasoned with salt and pepper, and browns it in a large iron skillet with lots of lard.

When it's crispy, she puts it into a roaster and lets it bake for about one and a half hours at 325 degrees. It comes out very tender. She then makes rich gravy, and we pour it over freshly mashed potatoes that are also grown on the farm.

It's strawberry season, so we have fresh strawberry shortcake for dessert. Grandma makes her strawberry shortcake with baking powder biscuits. She puts fresh smashed strawberries, sweetened with sugar, over the biscuits, and then she tops all this with homemade whipped cream.

When strawberries are out of season, she serves ice cream, made with a hand-cranked freezer. It takes a while, and we all take turns putting crushed ice and salt around the freezer and turn the crank until the ice cream is thick.

After dinner, we wash all of the dishes by hand. We did not have a dishwasher because they were rare and considered a luxury. We tell bedtime stories, and Grandpa listens to the radio. Television was just being invented, only in black and white and rather fuzzy.

Grandma then hustles us upstairs to the bedrooms where we're to sleep. We cuddle up under large homemade quilts. The cousins then begin to tell spooky ghost stories until Grandma warns us to be quiet, or we will get a spanking for staying up all night. (Yes, then you could get a spank on the butt.) She yells up, "Remember the rooster is going to get you up at six o'clock in the morning with his cock-a-doodle-doo!"

We finally settle down and go to sleep. Before we know it, we hear *cock-a-doodle-doo,* and it's time to milk the cows again. This time, we stay in bed—we just can't make it out to the barn that early. We tell Grandpa we're just too tired because we talked too much. He understands, but we still feel a little guilty.

A Special Kind of Eggs

After a while, we get up and go downstairs. We have a big breakfast of bacon, eggs, fried potatoes, fresh milk, homemade bread, and homemade strawberry jam. The breakfast is cooked on Grandma's old-fashioned wood stove, so it tastes really good.

Sometimes she makes us pancakes on the wood stove too. These are made on a big iron grill placed on top of the Stove. They're very good, and she has maple syrup from her maple trees to pour over the pancakes. We eat a big breakfast and are excited to go see the farm animals.

After we do the dishes and sweep up all the crumbs on the floor, we go out to the barn to see the kittens again. Then we decide to go see the horses. We head for the horse barn and take turns riding the horses. One is very old, so he doesn't go very fast. But he's still a lot of fun. Then we go to the pens where there are all kinds of rabbits. There is a really pretty white rabbit, and we pet him. There's also a gray rabbit. The rabbits are nice and soft and look very fluffy.

Soon we hear Grandma calling us to come and get a pail to gather eggs in the chicken coop. We get the pail and go into the chicken coop. We're afraid in there because we have to reach under the chickens to get the eggs. We're afraid they will peck us, but actually we are brave enough to get most of them. They are very special eggs. Some are white, and some are brown.

We gather all the eggs, which taste delicious when they're fresh. You don't get fresh eggs at the store, and these are very fresh eggs! It's fun to gather them. Sometimes a hen will be sitting on eggs to hatch baby chicks, so we leave them for her to guard. She keeps them warm until the chicks hatch. They're really cute when they're a few days old and can hardly walk on wiggly legs. They remind me of Easter. We can pick them up, as long as we're careful with them.

Pigs and a Wagon Ride to the Creek

There are lots of other animals on the farm besides cows, horses, rabbits, and chickens. There's a goose or two and some pigs. We decide to go to the pig pen out behind the barn.

The pigs are very fat. They love to play in the mud and slop around and get dirty. Ugh! They are so big and ugly and grunt and grunt when they're eating. We had bacon this morning for breakfast, which came from parts of the pigs. Also, pork roasts come from parts of the pigs.

Grandpa has decided to load up the wagon. After he hitches up the horses, he will give us a ride in the wagon. The horses are very tall. Grandpa is going to take us down a path. Actually, he's going to take us down in the meadow alongside the cornfield, so we can look at the stalks and see how big the corn is getting to be.

If we're lucky, he'll continue the ride down by the stream that runs through the farm. We'll go fishing there tomorrow, he promises.

Grandpa is a very excellent farmer. In the fall, the fields are stripped down of stalks and grow only grass the next year. Then the fields are planted with some other crop. This is called field rotation, and it helps to conserve the nutrients in the soil.

Surprise! Grandpa circles around the creek again. He says because it's such a hot day, we can go wading in the creek. We think this is wonderful because we are all very hot and sweaty by this time. We have shorts on, so we don't need to worry about getting our clothes wet.

We pick a shallow part of the creek where we can just walk across. We wade and splash each other and yell and scream. So much for not getting wet! We are completely soaked from head to foot.

Grandpa says, "Hope you don't get into trouble for getting so wet. But if you do, remind Grandma she used to do the same thing." He was laughing, so we figured we were pretty safe. He would put in a good word for us with Grandma and Mother also.

Back in the Fall

The sun is going down, so Grandpa helps us into the hay wagon and takes us back to the farmyard. Soon we must leave, but what a wonderful time we had with Grandpa and Grandma and our cousins. Grandpa and Grandma invite us back again in the fall when it's time to harvest the corn and gourds.

The farm is very beautiful in the fall. It's the time when the leaves turn all different colors: bright red, brilliant orange, and golden yellow. Grandma promises we can each pick a pumpkin for a jack-o-lantern. We'll have sweet corn, homemade pumpkin pie, and fresh apple pie in the fall. Since they have apple trees we help pick the apples.

Grandma promises us blueberry muffins and blueberry jam from the blueberries she's picked in the woods. It's a hard job to pick blueberries, as the mosquitoes are usually thick where berries grow. Grandpa and Grandma say that we should come back and help them later in the fall, and we'll have a great feast. My favorite is when we make a bonfire and roast wieners.

We give them a big hug, hop in our station wagon, and off we go back to the city. We are all fast asleep in the car because we're so tired from the fresh air and the wonderful time. I think my mother likes it when we sleep on the way home. She says it gives her some peace.

We get home, and Grandpa calls and asks when we're coming to see them. We laugh because we just left, but it does make us feel very good that he wants us to come back so soon.

And we are really looking forward to it.

Christmas Story by Grandma Dee Dee

This is a story about a little eight-year-old girl. It was the night before Christmas, and everybody was sleeping very soundly. Of course the girl was having trouble sleeping because she hadn't opened her presents on Christmas Eve.

The family was waiting until Christmas morning when Grandma and Grandpa would be coming in from out of town. Normally, they opened their presents on Christmas Eve, and she was very curious after seeing all the packages: silver, with a big red satin bow, blue, with snowflakes and a green bow, and a small, long, and narrow package with Santa wrapping on it.

One package had reindeer on it, and another rattled when she shook it. She was waiting to see if she was going to receive her favorite doll from Aunt Pauline—the one with black hair, red dress, and red shoes. She'd seen it at Dayton's Department Store, and she was hoping she'd get that doll!

On this night, the little girl was sleeping upstairs because her parents were sleeping downstairs with the new baby. They wanted to be sure to hear the baby if he cried. She heard a terrible noise in the kitchen, so she sneaked out of her cozy warm bed and tiptoed down the long winding staircase.

She peeked around the corner and thought, *My goodness, what could be happening in the kitchen?* It was a terrible racket!

Eggs and Potatoes and Lollipops Dancing

The open kitchen was next to the living room where the Christmas tree was standing. She crept carefully around the refrigerator. My goodness! What did she see? She saw one of the little white eggs dancing with the baked potato! They were dancing up and down the orange countertop, having a very, very good time.

Dancing and winding and twirling around and then doing the splits; they were having a good time, dancing to rock and roll! Since her mother hadn't cleaned up very well, they slipped in the gravy, and the gravy went splish-splash. There was gravy on the counter, and the baked potato almost went over the edge and became a smashed potato. The egg grabbed hold of the potato and pulled it back on the counter, and they began to dance again.

Pretty soon, the little girl heard another ruckus. All the lollipops had jumped out of their bowl (where her mother had put them). They all started to do a little dance, swinging their legs and doing steps like you see in Hollywood movies. They were swinging back and forth—one, two, and three.

One, two, three—skip!
One, two, three—kick!

One, two, three—kick!
One, two, three—hop!
One, two, three—hop!

A yellow lollipop, an orange one, a chocolate-mint one, a raspberry one, and a strawberry one too. They were circling and circling around and having the best time.

Cookies and Angels and a Rocking Horse All Prancing

Pretty soon, she looked to the right, and off came the cookie jar lid. All the chocolate chip cookies jumped out and started to swing and dance! They were having an extremely fun time, swinging and laughing.

The Christmas tree was glowing brightly. Suddenly, the angel light on the top of the tree came on and lit up all the decorations. Then they jumped off the tree! The little rocking horse jumped down and began to rock. A little mouse hopped down and jumped on the back of the rocking horse. A small kitten ornament jumped down too, but she decided she didn't want to dance, so she curled up with her big fuzzy tail right under the Christmas tree.

Then, all of the ornaments with pretty bulbs formed a line, and they began to dance: a bright gold ornament, a silver one, and another silver one with pink stripes. The tinsel began to glisten as all sorts of decorations began to dance.

A dancing teddy bear hopped off the tree and danced with its momma teddy bear. A little stuffed stocking jumped down, and everything popped out of the stocking!

Delores (Dee) Ray

Kittens and Piggies and Popcorn on Strings

A ball rolled out. Another kitten rolled out and went to lie down with the first kitten. The tiny bells on the tree were all jingling. When she looked over at the chimney where the stockings were hung, the little girl saw all of them singing and dancing. One stocking held a jack-in-the-box, and it popped open. Another stocking had a little piggy in it that said, "Oink, oink!"

The entire living room was alive with dancing! All of a sudden, she went back into the kitchen where she found some scrambled eggs left in the frying pan. The scrambled eggs turned into a little ball and jumped out of the pan. They began to dance on little legs and wore little hats made from chips of eggshell. They were all having a really fun time!

The popcorn began to pop in the microwave. The door flew open, and all the popcorn jumped out. The scrambled eggs hopped over to the sewing basket and got a ball of string and a sewing needle. The popcorn ran to the needle, strung itself, and then ran right over to the Christmas tree.

The popcorn jumped on the Christmas tree and hung itself all over the tree. It was very, very pretty—all decorated with popcorn and tinsel. The angel looked down and smiled.

These Are a Few of My Favorite Things—Oops! A Cough!

Suddenly the little girl said, "Oh!" She coughed, saying, "Uh oh!" The ornaments quickly jumped back on the tree. The scrambled egg jumped back onto the frying pan, and the egg jumped back into the carton. The baked potato fell back in the bowl, and everything became perfectly still. The popcorn, however, stayed on the Christmas tree—much to her surprise.

The little girl said to herself, *Am I dreaming, or did this really happen? I know I'll never tell anybody about this because no one will ever believe me. I can hardly believe it myself.*

She hopped back into bed and said, "That was so entertaining! At least it helped pass the night away, and now it won't be so long until I get to open my Christmas presents! I wouldn't have missed that for anything."

She threw her covers over her head, turned on her electric blanket, and fell fast asleep. Pretty soon, her mother was waking her. "Get up, get up. I can't believe you've overslept!"

The little girl just looked at her and smiled. She got up quickly and ran to the tree. By this time, the little girl had a completely different outlook. She looked at those little ornaments on the tree and thought, *Oh, do we have a secret!*

Her mother looked at her and asked, "So when did you make the popcorn strings? What a nice surprise." Her daughter just smiled.

Her mom thought, *My, this child is really acting strangely.*

The little girl, however, was thinking, *I'll always remember this as one of the merriest Christmases I've ever had!*

Amanda and Her Friend

This story is for Amanda, and it's a story about a white bunny. This little white bunny is very fluffy and very soft. He has pink ears—extremely pink. The little bunny has very, very long whiskers. He has a little pink nose that goes twitch, twitch, twitch every time he sees Amanda.

Amanda likes the little white rabbit to come and play with her. She likes him to watch *Sesame Street* with her while he's cuddled up next to her. As they watch, the little white rabbit says, "Amanda, please pet me, please pet me."

So Amanda remembers to be nice to the little white bunny. She puts her little hand on his head and says, "Nice bunny, nice bunny. I'm so happy to have you play with me and help me watch *Sesame Street*. It's so much fun that I want you here every day to play with me!"

Amanda likes going to town with her mother, JoAnn, who is a nurse. She gets to sit in her car seat. She likes sitting in her car seat because it's nice back there, and she has the whole back seat to herself. She gets to look out of the windows while her mother drives her around.

A Trip to the Video Store

They go to see Amanda's Daddy. He owns a video store where Amanda has been going ever since she was a couple of weeks old. She gets to pick out her own movies and everything!

One day, Amanda was especially lonely for her little white bunny rabbit. She knew her mother would not let the bunny rabbit ride in the car. But for some reason, Mommy forgot something in the house and left the car door open. The little white bunny jumped into the car, hopped in the back seat, and hid under Amanda's blanket.

Amanda giggled happily. She thought to herself, *I hope Mother doesn't see the little bunny rabbit. He's going to come with me to the video store that my daddy owns.*

The little white rabbit snuggled really close and kept still—so still that you could hardly hear him breathe. He stayed that way until her mother shut the door and took off.

They drove to the video store, and Amanda's mother didn't know the rabbit was there until she went to pick Amanda up. She was so shocked to see the little bunny rabbit. Bunny just smiled at her with a look that said, "This was such a nice ride!"

What could she do? She had to pick up the little white bunny and bring him into the store because it was too cold to leave him in the car. There were many customers inside, and they all said, "Oh! Is this the Easter Bunny? It's such a nice bunny!" There were children in the store who were extra happy to see the little white bunny.

Eggs!

The little bunny thought, *My goodness, I'm not used to getting all this attention. Not only that, but they think I'm the Easter Bunny. They think I can lay eggs. Yellow eggs, purple eggs, and blue eggs! Oh my goodness. I'm going to have a lot to live up to!*

The little bunny looked at Amanda and said, "Amanda, Amanda, Amanda, you are going to have to help me make all these eggs at Easter time!"

Amanda just leaned over and whispered in the little bunny's ear, "I will, I will, I will help you at Easter time! We'll make orange eggs, and we'll make purple eggs, and we'll make yellow eggs, and we'll make red eggs and striped eggs! We'll make one for Aunt Cindy, one for Uncle Ronnie, one for Uncle Bob & Aunt June, and one for Aunt Dee Dee. We'll make one for Grandmother Esther and one for Daddy Joey and Mommy Jo Ann! We'll make one for my puppy, Brandy!" Amanda went on and on. "We'll make one for cousins Rhonda and Jody and for all the children in the video store."

The little bunny just looked at Amanda and said, "My goodness, Amanda, you have so many relatives! You're such a lucky girl. I wish I had a lot of relatives like that. I'm the only one in my family, so it's nice that I can come into a big family like yours!"

Pals Forever

And so Amanda gave the little bunny a hug and said, "We will be pals forever, and we'll make the best Easter eggs that anyone has ever seen! That's our secret. We'll help the Easter Bunny out, because the Easter Bunny is going to be so busy this year!"

So that was their secret. Lo and behold, come Easter, that's exactly what they did. She helped the little bunny, and, together, they happily made all kinds of beautiful colored eggs. Amanda dyed them, and the little white bunny decorated scenes on them with his whiskers and his nose.

They were very special Easter eggs indeed. It was the best Easter Amanda had ever had. They were happy because they had made so many other people happy at Easter.

The little rabbit looked up at Amanda and said, "Thank you, Amanda, thank you! You've made me so happy. I hope you like me as much as you like Bert and Ernie from your favorite television show, Sesame Street. Well do this again next year."

The White Fawn

Brandy was born in early spring. His mom and dad had picked out his name several months beforehand in anticipation of his birth. Brandy seemed like a great name for a tiny little fawn.

But no one was expecting a new baby fawn to be pure white! Indeed, it was a tremendous shock, and word spread quickly throughout the forest. Soon, every creature in the forest came to take a peek at him. The little white furry rabbits loved him, as he was the same color as they were. The rabbits were very kind to Brandy, but some of the animals in the forest broke out in laughter when they saw him.

This saddened Mother Deer, and she began to cry. A little white rabbit spoke up and told her how much the rabbits loved him. Pretty soon, all the other rabbits gathered around Brandy and agreed that he was the most handsome fawn they have ever seen. And they had seen a lot of newborn fawns! Many of them had been living in the same forest for many years.

That cheered up Mother Deer. She began to smile and thanked them for being so kind to her and her family. Baby

Rabbit was jumping up and down so much that Mother Deer asked, "What is it you wish to tell me that you seem excited about?"

Mother Deer explained that she'd never thought of that but indeed Baby Rabbit was absolutely right. During hunting season, Brandy will blend right in with the snow and hunters will have a hard time spotting him. It made Mother Deer very happy that her baby would be out of danger.

Making Fun!

All summer long as Brandy was growing up, the other deer made fun of him for being pure white. Because Brandy was brave and kind, he swore he would never be cruel like that to any animal in the forest.

Mother Deer had a friend who had her own fawn around the same time Brandy was born. It looked like all the other fawns. The friend repeatedly told Mother Deer how perfect her own fawn was and that it was too bad that Mother Deer had such an ugly son.

Father Deer overheard what she was saying and asked her to stop visiting them if she didn't know how to be gracious and kind. He reminded her that friends don't make cruel comments. This made her very angry, and she stomped away with her nose in the air.

Brandy was actually handsome and special, just like his mother thought, even though he didn't look like all the other fawns.

It so happened that fall came around quickly, and Brandy and the other fawns began to grow antlers. Brandy's were as white as the rest of him!

With fall comes hunting season, and the hunters were out in droves. The other little fawn was spoiled and naughty and didn't mind his mom very well. He was warned that hunting season was a dangerous time and that he had to stay close to home. But he became curious and strayed farther out than he should have. Come dinnertime, his mother went looking for him but couldn't find him.

She was scared and began to cry. Soon, other deer and fawns began trying to help her find him. When they came to the edge of the forest, they would go no farther. They knew they would surely be shot by a hunter. They told the lost fawn's mother that the only one who could help her was Brandy because he was as white as the snow and wouldn't be seen.

They were worried though; they reminded her about how very cruel she had been to Brandy. They told her that he most likely would not help her find her son—not only because of how mean she'd been to him but because her own fawn had also been cruel to Brandy. He'd told Brandy he'd never fit in and would always be an outcast.

It was her only hope of ever seeing her son again though, so she decided to ask.

A Mother's Request

As she approached the edge of the forest, she saw Brandy's mother and father but not Brandy. She quickly ran up to them and asked where Brandy was. They thought it was very strange that she was looking for their son, since she never seemed to like little Brandy before. They said, "He's right over there. You just can't see him because he blends in with the snow."

"Oh! I see him now," she exclaimed. She explained her predicament and asked if they would allow him to help her find her son.

Mother Deer said, "You mean, you're asking our son to risk his life to save your son's life after making fun of him all summer?"

She answered, "I know, and I'm so ashamed of my behavior."

Father Deer said, "No way!" And at that, the worried mom burst forth in tears.

Finally, after what seemed like a hundred years of silence, Mother Deer said, "I'm definitely against it, but you can ask Brandy yourself. Father and I will leave it up to Brandy as to whether or not he wants to risk his life for someone who taunted him all summer."

The other mom approached Brandy with her head hung low, full of shame. She felt very humbled indeed. She explained the situation as Brandy listened very politely and without interruption, like the kind little fawn that he was. He looked her deeply in the eyes as she held her breath. She hardly dared to hope that he would say yes. "Of course I will help you," he replied.

Now or Never!

After all the abuse and malicious teasing Brandy had endured, she could hardly believe her ears. She thanked him, and he reminded her that he could only try to look for her son. But he didn't really know if he would be able to find him.

As Brandy started his search, he saw many hunters. Fortunately, however, they didn't notice him, since he was white as the snow. Brandy knew he didn't have much time; it would soon be dark. Then it would be too late, especially if the fawn had been shot.

The snow was getting deeper and deeper, and he wouldn't be able to go much further. He was about to turn back when he heard a light whimper and saw a movement. Heading that way, he saw the fawn.

He'd been wounded, but he was so happy to see someone he knew. He couldn't walk because of his wounds, and he was afraid the few remaining hunters would see him. Brandy locked his little antlers around one of the fawn's hooves and started to drag and push him to safety.

His wound was starting to bleed more, and by morning, hunters would surely find him. Brandy was feeling very exhausted himself. After all, he was just a little guy too. He figured if they reached the end of the forest by dusk, the bigger deer could come out and not be seen so easily.

Sure enough, as he approached the edge of the forest, the bucks all came out to help. Both mothers were ecstatic to see their sons.

Brandy made it to the edge of the forest and fell in a heap. It had been a hard and dangerous mission for such a little fawn. His parents took him home to rest and told him how proud they were of him and how brave he was. He barely heard them as he fell into a deep sleep.

By morning, the whole forest had heard about his brave act. They waited for him to wake up and then praised him endlessly. The little white baby rabbit reminded everyone that he had predicted this, and they all gave Brandy a badge for bravery.

The whole forest celebrated for two weeks. Brandy became famous throughout the land—so famous that even some hunters heard the story. They too honored him by placing a beautiful plaque in their lodge, and they made a law that no hunter could shoot a white deer.

And so it remains.

Christmas Cookies

Baking Christmas cookies was always so much fun with my mom. She informed me early one morning that it was time to bake Christmas cookies and asked if I wanted to help.

Well, I was busy reading a very good book and didn't want to put it down. But I knew that it would be a fun time to learn from her. I knew also that I must go at once. She was so fast that if I didn't put the book down immediately, I would miss my chance to have some fun baking cookies.

She seemed to do things faster than the blink of an eye. I recalled finishing a chapter in a book one time before going to the kitchen to bake a pie, and there it was—already done and in the oven.

Step One: Making Cookies

We had a large family of five girls and two boys, so there was always lots of activity in our home.

I was, however, like an only child in a way because I was further in age from the others. This was because a child before and after me had died when they were born. This sad fact would often make me feel very much alone, so when my mom said I could make cookies with her, I was happy indeed.

Well, to start, she put more wood in the stove and put a thermometer in the oven to gauge the temperature for baking the cookies. You see, when I grew up, we had these big stoves that used wood to cook and heat with. So she'd fire up the oven to get it ready to bake the cookies. How she could get it just right and get the cookies to bake just the way she wanted them—without burning—was absolutely amazing to me.

First, we got out the flour, which had to be sifted three times before we started the cookies. We didn't use mixes; these were truly homemade and delicious.

Then we got out the vegetable shortening and mixed that in very well. Next came the sugar, vanilla, and whatever flavor we were making. Last, we would add chocolate chips to make chocolate chip cookies or raisins and oatmeal if we were making oatmeal cookies.

This time, since we were making cookies for Christmas, we made several kinds. We made some called thumbprints, and in the middle we placed a chocolate kiss. For some, she would place a teaspoon full of homemade jam in the center of each cookie. Then we made some filled with cooked figs.

We also made some chocolate cookies, and then we'd frost them with homemade white and chocolate frosting. This day, I got to frost the cookies. Also, I got to lick out the remaining frosting in the bowl. Yummy—how fun!

My favorite was Russian teacakes. It was a fun name for me, as my father was of Russian descent. In fact, my grandfather, who once lived in Austria, was an Austrian lord.

That's why I found baking the teacakes so traditional and enjoyable. They were fun to make and to eat. I should mention that my mom was mostly Swedish, and Swedish people love to bake.

We made round balls and rolled them in powdered sugar. They are called Russian Tea Cakes. These could only be baked in a short time. Soon, the kitchen smelled very good. We pulled a cookie sheet out, and in the meantime, the ones we had prepared were ready to go in the oven so as not to waste our time.

We spread wax paper out on the counter, and when the cookies had cooled a bit after being taken out of the oven, we rolled them in powdered sugar and put them on the wax paper to cool completely. What a pretty sight this made! They couldn't be put in the cookie jar until they had cooled off completely, or they'd stick together and not look pretty.

Step Two: Eating Cookies!

Of course, we had to sample each kind. My father soon appeared on the scene and smelled them cooking; he loved sweets. My mom put a fresh pot of coffee on the stove to boil, and my father was soon sitting at the table with a big mug of coffee in front of him. He would always put two heaping spoons of sugar in his coffee. My mom placed a plate of fresh cookies in front of him.

My brothers and sisters came in from cutting down a fresh Christmas tree in the snow and were happy to see those cookies. So they all had some too. It was a wonder we had any left to put in the cookie jar!

After everyone had their treats, my dad helped them to place the Christmas tree in a stand and put it in the living room—not too close to the wood heater, or the tree would dry out and the needles would drop. We all helped to carefully put on colored lights and tinsel by hand—one by one—so that the tree would look nice (as my mother insisted).

My mom also helped, and she loved to sing "Silent Night" while we decorated the tree. I thought it was lovely to hear her sing, as I couldn't carry a tune myself. She had a beautiful voice. My dad got a ladder and placed a pretty angel on top of the tree. Meanwhile, looking out the window, the snow was lightly falling and looked beautiful on the evergreen trees.

When we were finished, my mom went back into the kitchen and put the cookies into several cookie jars to keep for the next day. I knew she would also deliver some to all the folks who were alone in our neighborhood. My mom and dad were very kind and generous people and were always thinking of others. What a great way to start the Christmas season!

Christmas with Grandma and Grandpa

It was a crisp, cold day in Minnesota. Wearing cuddly flannel pajamas, I had just awakened under a big down quilt made by my grandma. I was sitting there, thinking and thinking because it wasn't time to get up yet. Everybody was still asleep in my grandpa and grandma's house where I was visiting. So I lay there and thought and thought.

I was looking out of the window, thinking, *What a beautiful sight out there!* It was still very dark, as if it was the middle of the night. It was snowing, and I thought it was beautiful. Then I realized that somehow the window had been left open, and the snowflakes had fallen on the floor near my bed. I thought I should close my eyes and see what I could do to make myself small enough to get out of the window.

Before I realized it, I was walking on the snowflakes, having a grand time. Suddenly, I was walking on the moon beam and swinging on the stars and seeing some clouds that were invisible from earth. I was looking at the clouds and laughing with the clouds, which no one else knew were there.

I played and danced for a long time. Swinging on the stars was such fun—swinging from one to the other. Very quickly, I realized that it was getting close to early morning, so I swung down to the pine forest next to my grandparents' farm. The pine trees were all lightly dusted with snow, and the ground was glistening as though it had glitter sprinkled on it.

The fir trees reminded me of music boxes. They were decorated with red cardinals, all chirping and saying, "Come on, Nicole! Good morning, Nicole! We were waiting for you. We want to show you our beauty. We have decorated the whole forest just for you!"

With that, a squirrel came around one of the trees. He had a beautiful long tail that made swish marks in the snow. He looked up at me and handed me one of his acorns with a smile. He chatted, "Merry Christmas!"

After that, a little chickadee came and perched on a nearby branch. He glanced at me and said, "Nicole, I'm going to sing you a Christmas song!" So he sang "Merry Christmas" to me in three different tones.

A little farther into the forest, a family of beautiful deer was standing in a clearing. They looked at me, and they were very, very pleasant too, with their big brown soft eyes and little white tails. They said, "We will run a race for you. You can enjoy watching us!" So they ran around in the forest—dashing here and there—having a wonderful time entertaining me.

The mother (doe) won the race. She was a beautiful golden brown color. The father deer (buck) was beautiful too, and he had the most magnificent rack of horns I've ever seen. What a sight!

Soon, we were walking over a little stream. There was a little man there who was ice fishing. He was trying to catch a nice fish for his family to fry for dinner.

I began to realize then that it was getting very late. Somebody in the house might be up by now. So I scrambled back to my bed and snuggled under the covers. Someone knocked at my door. Grandpa was there. He said, "Come on, Nicole. I've lit the fire, and I'm going to read you a story while Grandma makes our breakfast."

So there I was, curled up in my Grandpa's arms. I had the nicest Grandpa; his name was James. He was kind of cuddly and warm. He had gray curly hair and glasses that sometimes fell down on his nose. He loved children and would always tell me the best stories. He would play with me. I loved it when he made popcorn for me. He would often play the piano just for me and also taught me how to play the piano. He was a great musician. Every day, he dressed in his business suit, but he also liked to wear his cowboy boots. In the wintertime, he liked to wear his flannel shirt at home.

Grandma liked to cook, and she was out there cooking now. Sometimes Grandpa would cook too. He made the best waffles; they were my very favorite. He served waffles with syrup that he had made. They were so good that I could eat lots of them.

I always had such a good time at Grandpa and Grandma's. They would light the fire in the fireplace and would lie on the soft sheepskin rug in front of the fireplace. They would let me be myself and made me feel happy and wanted. We would sing songs and laugh a lot.

The house was filled with warmth and love. It was the perfect place to visit during the holidays. I will always remember those special nights. When it was time for bed, I knelt down and thanked God for my wonderful family and for all the warmth and happiness. I prayed that every child would know that same warmth, and if they didn't have it, they would know that all they had to do is go within and say, "Jesus, please come and help me. I need your comfort and your love." I wanted them to know that he would always be there for them.

I hoped that all of the children in the world would have a very Merry Christmas and that they could have a grandpa and grandma as wonderful as mine.

Merry Christmas to all!

My Friend the Grasshopper

It was kind of a lonely, sad day, and I was feeling very bored. I thought, *What can I do to have some fun?* I laid down on the couch and thought, *What if I could become small?* The first thing I knew, I was about as small as an ant, so I thought to myself, *Now that I am as small as an ant, what can I do this afternoon that will be exciting?*

I looked out the window and saw that it was raining, I thought, *If it's raining and I am as small as an ant, I had better be careful about what I do because an ant is very, very little. I will have to be very, very careful!* I knew I could make myself big again, but I wanted to stay small for a while. I thought and thought and thought!

Just as I was thinking about it, my friend the grasshopper hopped by the window and looked in. He seemed to be smiling at me and telling me to come over by the window. I went to the window, and he seemed to say, "Why don't you hop on my back?" I said, "I'm afraid of the raindrops." He said, "Oh don't worry, don't worry. Just hop on my back. I will take care of you."

I thought, *Gee, that really sounds exciting!* So I decided to hop on the grasshopper's back. He went hop-hop and happily hopped. "Just hang on now, and hang on to this umbrella that I made out of a leaf for you," he said.

We went out in the fields under the corn. It really looked funny under the corn, like a big forest of corn. It was rather hot there, so he said, "Why don't you put on your magic wings, and we can fly above all this?"

"I'm afraid of getting wet," I answered.

"Just hang on to the umbrella," he said.

So he put on his magic wings, and we went flying.

Lo and behold! A grasshopper can go in between the raindrops. I never once got wet, even though I lost the leaf umbrella when I grabbed for his neck because I thought he was going to run into a raindrop.

We went to visit my girlfriend. I could see that she was in her house, playing with her doll. I thought, *Boy will she be surprised when I tell her at school tomorrow that I saw her playing with her doll.* She was putting on the pink dress and the shiny white shoes. She looked really bored. We had our noses right up to the window, but she didn't even notice us.

We flew off again and went with the magic wings through the raindrops to another friend's house. The truth be told, the grasshopper had borrowed the wings from his friend the dragon fly. No wonder they sparkled so much. My boyfriend, John, was playing with his train set and wouldn't go outside either. He would be so surprised if I told him about this in school tomorrow. Then I realized that he wouldn't believe me anyway. Sometimes you have to keep secrets to yourself, I decided.

It was so much fun with the grasshopper—hopping and flying around. We flew over some tree tops and buzzed by downtown St. Paul. We flew over the city of Minneapolis. We were up as high as the IDS Tower! The grasshopper said, "Hang on! Hang on!" We had a really exciting trip.

Then I said, "I think I want to go up among the clouds!" So we went right up among the fluffy white clouds and right through some of the clouds. What an experience!

Then we followed a bumblebee. He showed us a field with little violets. Then we flew over a high field of daffodils and hopped around on them for a while. All of a sudden, we slid off the daffodils, and the little bee brought us some honey tea. We had tea, sitting among the daffodils. It was so delightful! The flower is bright yellow like the sun. We sat our tiny tea cups on the little things that come out of the daffodil. We had honey with the tea, served on tiny little crackers. The bumblebee had supplied us with these tiny cups, so we sat on the daffodils and the breeze blew by and whispered "Hi." What a day!

I decided I had best get home because it was getting late. It had been a fun day, but I was getting tired from all of the excitement. My friends promised me we would go to fairyland on our next trip. I said, "Oh! That would be wonderful. Let's do it next week!" Perhaps next week, I will get to go and see the Fairyland folks. I hope, I hope, I hope!

Dressing Up

One day, I was visiting my aunt who lets me play grownup. I get to put on her high heels; they're three inches high!

I put on her silver heels and dress up in her long purple evening gown with sequins sewn all over it. I get to tramp around the house and it's a wonderful feeling! I like going up and down the stairs, pretending I'm in a beauty contest. You know, like the ones you see on TV.

I put on a great big hat with flowers all over it. What fun! I pretend that I get to go to a kiddy cocktail party. My aunt puts some 7 Up and a cherry in the glass I'm drinking out of.

Later on in the afternoon, we have ice cream and cookies. Toward evening, she lets me dress up in my own favorite dress, and we go to dinner.

Bubbles, Perfumes and Big, Fluffy Towels

But before we go to dinner, we must take a bath, and I hate taking baths. She said I could take a bubble bath and use all of her perfumes and powders. So, I decided that perhaps a bath isn't so bad after all.

My aunt has all kinds of special bubble baths. One kind has little pink seed-like things in it. You put it in the tub and run the hot water, and this makes all kinds of bubbles! It's the type that doesn't go away, so I get to sit in the bubble bath with all of these bubbles floating around. This makes taking a bath a lot of fun, even though I usually don't like taking baths at all.

While I am in the bubble bath, pretty music is playing. While I'm listening to the music, the bubbles just keep floating around. I daydream, and the bubbles just float around the top and splash up in the air.

My aunt always makes it really nice to take a bath, and I thought to myself, *This looks just like the ladies I see in the old movies taking bubble baths.* When I stood up and took a shower to get all the bubbles off, she let me use her shampoo. When I dried off, I put her dusting powder all over me with a big powder puff. Then I chose a pretty perfume and sprayed it behind my ears.

I dried my hair with my own fluffy blue towel. She'd had my name embroidered on the towel.

When I was done drying off, I put on my soft terry cloth robe. I put it up in the air with a dramatic flair, like I had seen in the movies. I could see my shadow against the bathroom wall, and I made little pictures on the wall with it. What a wonderfully relaxing time.

Soon, my aunt called me to dry my hair, but not too much. She said that blow-drying your hair too much can dry it out.

Needless to say, after all that, I was ready to go to my favorite restaurant to eat.

Halloween

It was Halloween. It happened to be one of those Halloweens that was just perfect for black cats, goblins, and haunted houses. Whee! I had decided to be a black cat because I had been a ghost the year before, and my feet stumbled over that sheet a number of times till it was grimy black all around the bottom. Besides that, by the time I got untangled, my friends seemed to be a mile ahead of me. Let me ask you, who wants to be left behind on a black haunted Halloween night? Too scary for me! So a cat it would be. I thought a cat would be nice because I could carry an umbrella. Also, the cat outfit would be warm on a cool evening when it was sleeting outside.

I went to meet my skunk friend, my raccoon friend, and my girlfriend Amy who always had to be really cute and dressed as a beautiful fairy with transparent wings. She carried a magic wand.

How I envied her; she always looked so beautiful with her blond hair, blue eyes, and long lashes. She wasn't like me—a freckle-faced redhead. Just the thought of it—ugh! No wonder I wanted to be a cat.

So we met at her house and decided to get on with a great night of trick or treating. The night was black, cloudy, and it was sleeting slightly. We were to meet the rest of the group on the corner of Fifth and Milton. When we met, my friend Roger said there was a new kid in town named Clint whom he had invited along. He was to meet us shortly. Roger said that Clint seemed nice, but no one else would talk to him. "He's from a foreign country. He must be Irish," Roger said, adding, "Mom always says to give a new kid a chance. You might even learn something from him. My mom is so wise."

Well, Clint soon arrived and, believe me, he was Irish. He had really bright red hair (even redder than mine—yippee!) and freckles all over his nose. Actually, I thought he was kind of cute—for a boy. He had the biggest grin I had ever seen and a mischievous look in his soft blue eyes.

Then I said, "I remember you. You pulled my hair!" He just laughed and gave me a wink. Of course, I blushed. I must admit he did seem nice and fun too. Besides, I liked the idea of someone with more red in his hair than I had and more freckles on his nose than I did.

Clint said, "Well, are we going to the old mansion?"

We said, "Which one?"

He said it was the one at the very top of the hill to the right of Laura Street.

We responded with, "We never go up there. We are afraid to."

He asked us why, and we told him about the old lady who lived up there. She is very mean! He asked us how we knew that if we had never been up there. "How would you really know if she is or isn't mean?"

That was a very good point! How did we know? After all, none of us had ever met her.

He said, "You Americans always have the weirdest ideas about things that you don't know anything about. Some castles are a lot of fun. We have a lot of them in Ireland that are haunted and are really, really fun! Some of them have nice ghosts."

We looked at him and could hardly believe what he was saying. He was so casual about ghosts!

"Are you really that afraid? Or are you ready for an adventure?" he asked.

Well, of course the boys said they weren't afraid. My friend Amy started to cry and get her fairy suit all wet.

Clint said, "Oh, you can stay here if you wish."

She said, "Oh, no, no, no!"

Finally, we calmed her down and decided to get on with it. We told Clint that on the way up we would have to cross the cemetery, climb a fence, and go over a brick wall. He said, "That sounds like fun."

We decided to go through the cemetery, as it was the shortest route up the steep hill to the old house. One of the boys said, "I should stop and visit my grandmother. She is buried over there."

We all went over and left a piece of candy on her tombstone and told her hello. The Irish boy said an Irish prayer for her. Gosh, we were learning a lot from this kid already.

We were all cold, but suddenly, the wind stopped, and it felt like we had warm sun shining on us. It was almost as if someone was smiling at us; we felt completely warm and cozy. We said good-bye to our friend's grandmother, and no one seemed to feel fearful any longer. We just had the feeling we would be all right.

One of the boys said, "You know, I remember when my grandma used to be friends with that lady up on the hill years ago. She went to school with her." We thought that was a good omen.

Then we went across the creek, and someone slipped. It was the boy dressed as a raccoon and was he ever wet! So, we had to stop and dry his clothes off a little bit, squeezing all the water out. We thought, *Now, for sure, he will get pneumonia!*

We put his clothes in one of our trick-or-treat bags, and each of us gave him some of our clothes (from what we were wearing under our outfits) so that he would have something dry to wear. He kept sneezing because we didn't have shoes or socks for him. When he walked, he went squish, squish, squish! The water was running out of his shoes. He really looked a wreck. We told him, "One good thing is, you will be able to miss a week of school!"

That went over big, as he was an "A" student. Besides, he said, "It is not fun being in the hospital."

He was right about that, I thought. I had been there once and it was a terrible experience. I was beginning to see his point of view. Somethings were indeed worse than school and Mrs. Firewhamp, our teacher.

We came to a field surrounded by a big barbed wire fence, and on the other side were cows that would go "moo!" I had forgotten that farmer Jones's land ran across there. When Miss Patti Perfect—Amy, I mean—went through the fence, she ripped her pants. I had to turn away because I wanted to laugh, but I didn't want to hurt her feelings. Because she was so embarrassed, I almost felt sorry for her. All in all, we finally helped each other get through the hole we had made in the fence. *Farmer Jones will love that,* I thought.

I said, "Let's rest here for a while and have a candy bar." While resting, we looked up and saw an owl! He had big green eyes. He was really beautiful. I thought, *Gosh, I have never been out on a Halloween like this before. I never saw an owl before either!* I think it's because they are night creatures. We hoped he wasn't vicious.

We walked and walked. Finally, we could see the mansion on the hill; it had one dim light on in the front entry, as if the old woman was expecting us. I said, "See, she is expecting us!"

We got closer, and after walking about a half mile, we came to a fence that was so creaky it scared us when we tried to open it. Finally, it came open with a big jerk, and in we were. We got up to the mansion, and it was awesome—just awesome.

Pretty soon, someone came out and grabbed one of the boys from behind and said, "I have got you now."

We were scared to death! Then he took off his mask and said, "Don't be afraid, don't be afraid! I'm just the gardener. Did you come for tricks and treats?"

We said, "Yes, we have come for tricks or treats."

He said, "Well, come on up then."

We said, "No, no, no! We can't; she will be angry with us!"

The gardener said, "Oh no, on the contrary, she will be happy to see you."

He had an awful time talking us into it. He said, "Well, if you're not really brave, you can come around to my house on the side. I'll make you some hot chocolate."

Being the cowards that we were, we decided his idea seemed like a good one. We went back to his house, which was just for the servants. He said, "Would you like to see the horses and the barn?"

We said, "Sure!"

He showed us the horses; they were beautiful riding horses. He showed us the old buggies and other interesting items in the barn. There was a sleigh for winter. We said, "My goodness, how do you keep this so shiny and new looking?"

He said, "Well, Mrs. Grayson has been waiting for years for some children to come by. She always says, 'Someday I know someone will love me enough to come by. I want to keep this all shiny and perfect just in case some children come to visit.'"

We thought, *All this time, we have been missing this. How wonderful everything is! We thought this lady was wicked! Indeed, it appears we were mistaken!*

The gardener said, "She isn't wicked at all. She is just, very lonely."

One of the boys said, "I think my grandmother used to be her friend."

The gardener asked, "What is your grandmother's name?"

He replied, "Her name is Maria."

"Yes," said the gardener, "they went to school together. They were the best of friends."

We told the gardener about the episode at the tombstone. He said, "Well, that is how they all got in trouble; they all believe in spirits. Mrs. Grayson believes in spirits. She believes there are many good spirits. Years ago, she used to tell fortunes, and people considered it to be evil. They were so mean to her that she had to stay in her house. When she went down into town, they would throw stones at this lovely lady.

"She really *is* a wonderful lady. She has always been friendly with your grandmother. The two women seem to communicate back and forth. She probably knows you are coming because that warmth in the cemetery was a good omen. They have always been able to communicate. She felt that your grandmother was close at hand and protective of her. That is probably why you felt so good!"

He told us all about it, and we were then really ready to meet her. The gardener took us up the flagstone steps and rang the doorbell. It opened, and the most pleasant looking lady you would ever want to meet appeared. We could smell ginger cookies and apple cider. She invited us in, and we all gathered around a big, round oak table with gigantic chairs. We told stories all night and had the best time! She showed us around the house, which had huge rooms. When we were seated comfortably in the living room, she said, "Yes, I live here with a ghost, but he is a friendly ghost."

Our eyes popped wide open. She smiled at our astonishment. The Irish boy didn't seem surprised at all. He actually wanted to meet the ghost. He was the most interesting boy I had ever met. I was really beginning to like him—that is, for a boy.

It was getting late; Mrs. Grayson asked if we could stay overnight. We said that we would have to call our parents and ask permission. We called and told our parents that we were trick or treating. I said I was with John and Timmy. Timmy said he was with me. Strangely enough, none of our parents seemed the least bit worried. We did not get the usual third degree. It was truly a first. None of them asked whose house we were going to be staying at.

So we stayed overnight. Our hostess said, "Now remember: if something happens during the night, don't worry because he's a friendly ghost. He might take you for a ride or rock your bed, or he might tickle your nose with a feather. He might also play some music on the piano or upset your water jar or take your shirt. But don't worry; he is very friendly. And after you are here for a while, you might be able to talk with him. He'll blow on your nose if he means yes, or he will flicker the lights."

We thought, *Oh this will be fun and absolutely perfect for Halloween!*

One of the boys asked, "Did my grandmother tell you we were coming?"

"Yes, she did. Didn't you notice that she was at the table with us?" she asked.

"I thought I felt someone tap my shoulder and kiss me lightly on the cheek," the boy answered.

Mrs. Grayson said, "You can be sure that was her." She then added, "John and Clint can stay in the attic room. You two other boys can stay in the blue room. And you two girls can stay downstairs next to me, in case you get frightened."

The boys—except for Clint—pointed their fingers at us and said, "Fraidy cats!" Clint was much too polite to do that. This, to me, was just amazing.

We all took to our rooms, promising to exchange stories at breakfast. Patty Perfect and I went into the room next to Mrs. Grayson. Of course, she took out the nicer pair of pajamas. I like pink, but she also likes pink. She took the pink ones, and I thought, *Oh well, I will just go over and pick up the yellow pajamas.*

Suddenly, the pink ones flew right at me, as if I was meant to put them on. We were both astonished! So I got to wear the pink ones. I thought, *This is an interesting ghost!*

He pinched Patti Perfect, and she yelped. I thought, *Good for you, ghost! She is such a spoiled little brat. I'd like to pinch her myself at times!* She didn't cry; that was unusual in itself. We decided it was time to hop in bed. The covers were way down at the bottom of the bed; it was the most gigantic one I'd ever seen.

Suddenly, the covers flew over us. We both laughed and said "Oh—this is fun!"

We lay there watching the moon in the distance. All of a sudden, it was like the moon just moved right to our window, and moonbeams came streaming in. I glanced up, and there was a tiny fairy dancing on the moonbeams. A little orchestra was playing on the biggest moonbeam. They jumped off the moonbeam, dropped down to the floor, and proceeded to have a party. They were all dressed like elves and started playing ring-around-the-rosy and throwing flowers up in the air. Pretty soon, they had a little pumpkin with a black cat on it. That was their sign for us to understand they knew it was Halloween. They entertained us for half an hour.

All of a sudden, a wind came up, and the light in the pumpkin blew out. The moonbeams drifted back up to the moon, and it was pitch black—coal black. We heard a lot of creaks and whoops, and a bat flew across my head. I jumped under the covers and thought, *Oh my, I hope the ghosts are just playing tricks on us!*

We heard some moans and groans, and when we peeked out from under the covers, we saw a light, smoky thing going above the bed. A witch face came down and bonked me on the head. I looked at Patti Perfect. I could barely see her well enough to make out her face. She was absolutely terrified, frozen stiff, and completely speechless! I thought, *What is happening now? Okay, ghost, that's enough!*

With that, we heard a loud roar and laughter; the room became immediately bright again with moonlight. As I fell fast asleep, I wondered what the boys were going through. We slept and slept and slept like we had never slept before. It was as if we were lying on a wonderful feather bed.

All of a sudden, I felt a double twitch of my nose and a hot breath on my ear. I saw my clothes come flying toward me. That meant the ghost wanted me to get up, so I obeyed, got up, and got dressed. Patti Perfect stayed there. The door opened, and she was still sleeping. I thought to myself, *This is strange.*

I walked out the door. I could see another door open at the top of the stairs, so I walked up there very slowly. When I got up to the room, the light was already on.

I was in an attic room. As I walked in, the trunk popped open. Inside the trunk was the most beautiful doll I had ever seen. It was a bride doll, dressed in a long satin gown decorated with pearls. The doll had long brunette hair. It was very lovely indeed. There was also a groom doll, which I had rarely seen before. (I had mostly girl dolls.) I took both of them out and played with them for a long time; it was just so much fun. The room was filled with gold and lavender light.

Then, I noticed some books nearby. I picked one up; it was a book of fairy tales. I opened it and found my name there. I thought, *This book was printed in 1892, and my first name is printed on it!* It was as if it had belonged to me. I thought, *This is strange. I know I had an English aunt, and her name had been the same as mine. But what connection would that have to this book? It's all very interesting.*

I looked at the book and then looked at it again. All of a sudden, I glanced up, and there was Mrs. Grayson. I thought, *She is going to be angry with me.*

But she wasn't. She just smiled and laughed. She said, "That book has been here a long time. A friend of mine had a niece in England. She always said she had a beautiful niece she had never met. Not realizing America was so big, she moved here. She said to me, 'If you ever meet her, would you give her this book?' That's how I happen to have the book."

I said, "This book is so beautiful and elegant, with its leather cover, its name printed in gold, and all sorts of beautifully illustrated stories."

She said, "Yes, that would be a present with love." The book just glowed. She then said, "The book is yours."

I gave her a big hug and thanked her. Then she said, "Oh, I see you have found the dolls. A long time ago, I had those made up because my boyfriend jilted me. It took me many years to get over it. I was bitter, but I did eventually get beyond it, and now I am happy."

She said that she had always kept the dolls in memory of her love for that man. But now it didn't bother her anymore, so I could come and play with them anytime I wished. She added, "I guess I was not meant to be married. He went off and married someone else—not even a girl he was in love with—but that was years ago."

"This is the most interesting time I've had in a long while!" I said.

The door opened, and she said, "Apparently, my friend—the ghost who lives here—recognized you. This is the room you should have been led to. Let's go downstairs, and you can help me make breakfast."

We went downstairs. My friends were still sleeping. She gave me a huge apron to wear, one that went around my neck and had a top and bottom. You know how it is when you fry bacon; it always splatters on you. She gave me a little step ladder to stand on that had a Mother Goose design on it. She said I could fry the bacon but warned me not to get too close because the grease could get very hot and jump right out of the pan and on to my clothes. I laughed, agreeing with her.

Mrs. Grayson added, "We are going to have a great breakfast! Bacon, eggs, blueberry pancakes, homemade strawberry jam, and my favorite—hot chocolate! Later on, if you want to, we can make cookies. In fact, since it is the weekend, you can stay until tomorrow if you wish."

Soon we heard the other kids coming. They all vaulted into the kitchen just as the table was being set. They were so excited; they said they had a wonderful night. There were jumping jacks in their rooms, and just as they began to play the game, the window opened and shut all by itself! They said they'd had a fantastic time, but the strangest things happened to them.

Timmy said that he flew out of the window and back again. The other boy said he levitated right up to the ceiling. It was just like he was walking on air! He walked all over the house like that. The others said they had seen him in their room when it got pitch black, and the boys had seen the covers fly right over their heads.

The boys in the attic said they also had a wonderful time. All kinds of stuffed animals came to life in their room. They had a marvelous time with that. It was just like a picnic. They asked Mrs. Grayson, "Can we come back again?"

She replied, "I wouldn't have it any other way. In fact, now that Halloween is here, winter will be coming soon, and you can come back and have sleigh rides. Right now though, I do need someone to help me harvest my pumpkins and the rest of my vegetables."

We said we would be happy to help in exchange for sleigh rides. Then she said that we could come and ride the horses in the summer. We told her we had a friend who was disabled and almost never had a chance to get out into the sunshine and fresh air. We wondered if it would be appropriate to bring her with us. She said, "Maybe some laughter and buggy rides would help her feel better, so yes, bring her!"

We had a marvelous time all winter and into the summer visiting Mrs. Grayson. We brought our little friend up, and she laughed and laughed in the fresh air and sunshine. We took her for walks in the meadow by carefully supporting her. She went for buggy rides, and it was almost like a miracle happened. She kept getting stronger and stronger. The doctors could not believe what was happening. The ghost would pull her nose and tug at her hair. She became good friends with the ghost. (I do believe she was his favorite.)

All of us would work and laugh until the sun went down. It was fun helping Mrs. Grayson, and she so appreciated it. By the time school started again, our friend was almost able to walk. I wonder to this day if it was a miracle that she became so strong and healthy—just like the rest of us. We still think it was because of the sunshine and laughter and our friend the ghost of course. But for whatever reason, she became perfectly well.

The Irish boy, Clint, was right! Don't make judgments about people you don't know. Through our mutual friendships, we opened a beautiful world, one that enriched our childhoods by opening us up to new possibilities. We all had wonderful, unforgettable experiences.

The Poor Little Church Mice

P oor little church mice. They lived in a big white church with a big beautiful bell. The church was tumbling down, and the congregation was growing old. The church treasury was getting poorer and poorer and poorer.

The mice didn't know what they were going to do for another crumb. There was Momma Mouse, with her faded apron and bonnet with holes in it. Daddy Mouse had holes in his socks, and the clothes for Boy Mouse and Girl Mouse were ripped and tattered.

They were all extremely worried about what they were going to do to survive. They thought and thought and said, "We need a new, younger congregation. We need somebody to lead the congregation with inspiration. How in the world are we going to attract this person?"

Listening to God

One little boy mouse said, "I heard about this theory called meditation. People sit still, and then they go into silence. They wait and listen. They listen to hear God speak to them."

Daddy Mouse said, "You know, I think that's a pretty good idea because most people talk to God, but they don't listen. This just may be a very good answer, so let's try it tonight when it is very quiet and dark outside. Let's light our candles, and the whole family will hold hands and join in a circle. We will go into our inner selves. We will all meditate, and we will listen to see if God gives us an answer."

So that night, all of the little mice put on their slippers with holes in them, and they sat around a single lit candle. Some closed their eyes, and some looked directly into the candle light. But they were all silent. They listened and listened. This went on for about half an hour.

They were so silent that they could hear the wind blowing around the old church. It was very cold and snowy, and the wind was blowing into the cracks of the old white church, making the candle flicker, but it didn't go out. So after the half hour went by, they said, "One, two, and three! Now we will discuss what we heard."

James, the little Boy Mouse, said, "Remember that Mr. Jones's grandson is going to graduate from ministry school very soon. I understand he has some new, inspirational ideas."

Daddy Mouse said, "Well, when I was listening to God, somehow the words *prayer meeting* flashed into my mind. Maybe at a prayer meeting we could all hide under the pews where people sit. We could give them thought messages to hire this young man—Tommy, I believe, is his name,"

The others said, "Oh, they'll never give him a chance."

But Daddy and Mamma Mouse said, "We have to think positively.

It's definitely worth a try. After all, what do we have to lose? Let's try!"

Lighting Candles

So the mouse family crept in for the next Wednesday night prayer meeting. There was Mr. Jones, a tailor, with his horn-rimmed glasses, his old tailcoat, and a walking cane that went thump, thump, thump. There was Anne, the single lady, who was always looking for a husband. There was the widow, Sally, whose husband had been killed, leaving her with two little boys to support. There was the librarian, and there was Mr. Taylor, whose business was slowly going downhill. There was John, the watchmaker, and George, the jeweler. Other people were there, too: Mary, the housewife, Lois, the waitress at the local bar, and June, the schoolteacher.

As they sat and prayed in the twilight, for some reason, they decided to light candles. The mice thought this was interesting because candles had never been lit before at the Wednesday evening meeting. The mice were wondering if the congregation was trying to save on the electric bill or, if for some reason, they had gotten the message that candles help you to pray better.

When they had lit all of the candles, someone said, "Gee, why are we using candles? We usually just dim the lights."

June, the schoolteacher, said, "I just read in a book that candlelight is very effective in a prayer meeting, so I thought we should try it." They all agreed they wanted something new anyway.

As they were praying with their eyes closed, all of the mice put on their little slippers; they didn't want to be heard. Each one sat under someone's chair, and they said to themselves, *We will deliver messages. We will speak to the higher minds of these people and send messages encouraging them to hire Tommy.*

They did this through the whole prayer meeting. Just before the service ended, they all scurried back to their little holes and peeked out around the corners to watch what would happen next.

At the end of the meeting, one young lady said, "You know, I have the strangest feeling that we should hire Tommy. We need some new blood in this church. Maybe he will be inspirational. I hear that he has some good ideas on prosperity. Lord knows, this church could use some prosperity!"

Mr. Denopoli said, "Oh no. We can't afford him."

The others said as a group, "Well, let's try it. Let's take a vote!"

Mr. Jones said, "After all, Mr. Taylor, I understand that you could use some more business. Maybe we could all use some prosperity ideas."

So in spite of Mr. Denopoli's fussing and some moans and groans from a few others, they decided to vote.

They agreed to ask Tommy if he would be the assistant minister. It being his first job opportunity, he was more than delighted. He wasn't at all worried about the church being drafty and the bills piling up. He was anxious to try out his new methods and his beliefs.

The First Prayer Meeting

The first day Tommy was there, he sang loud. Everybody went out of there more inspired than ever. He just seemed to have a glow. Everybody thought happy thoughts, and they were very pleased with him. The regular minister no longer wanted to handle the prayer meetings because he was getting quite old, so he asked Tommy if he would mind taking over.

With a great deal of enthusiasm, Tommy replied, "Sir, I would be delighted to take charge of the prayer meetings on Wednesday evenings."

When the next prayer meeting came around, the little mice were very curious. They looked at Tommy and thought, "My, Tommy is so nice. He has such a pleasant smile and is so optimistic."

He told the people about some of his new ideas. They centered on positive thinking and doing one's best. He said if people practiced these things, God would help them succeed in their efforts. They just shook their heads and thought, "These are some of the strangest ideas we have ever heard! How could thinking like that ever help us make more money so that we can repair our church and buy new songbooks?"

Tommy patiently said to them, "What do you have to lose? In prayer, I want each of you to think of what you would like most for the church and for your personal lives. Then we'll share our ideas, and we'll encourage each other."

After the meeting, they sat around and Tommy said, "Now, what would someone like?"

Mr. Jones said, "Well, we could sure use some more business."

They all said they could use more prosperity. The widow, Sally, could use a better job and so forth and so on. So they decided they should try some of Tommy's ideas.

A couple of weeks went by, and nothing of substance happened. At the next prayer meeting, Tommy encouraged everyone to just keep trying because it would take practice and faith.

The next week, Mr. Jones came in and said, "You know, I needed to have six new suits brought in for alterations in order to break even and earn a little profit last week. I visualized six suits needing alternations. Lo and behold, a new lady moved into our neighborhood, and she brought me exactly six of her husband's suits for alteration because he'd lost thirty pounds."

The congregation thought that was very interesting. They were happy for Mr. Jones. Then the widow, Sally, shared her desire. "I want to get a job at the high school. It would be a big job and would earn me a couple of hundred dollars more a month, but I don't think I can get it."

The people said, "Well, why don't you prepare yourself for it anyway and try for it? What do you have to lose? After all, if you don't try, you can't possibly succeed. We'll all say prayers for you and visualize you getting it. See yourself accepting this new position. Let's practice Tommy's new ideas. After all, it worked for Mr. Jones, and it may just work for you."

Ask, Listen, and God Will Help

So Sally held her head high and went for the interview. She remembered the congregation and the new ideas Tommy was teaching them. She was the last person to interview for the position. She asked the congregation, "What chance do I have?"

They said she should keep up the positive thinking and visualize herself working at the school.

She said, "Why not? I *will* try it! Besides, I find it rather fun to think these new positive thoughts. They sure make me feel good."

The congregation continued to encourage her. A few weeks went by, and she said, "I still don't know if I have the job." They told her to remember to keep up the good, positive thoughts.

The next Wednesday night, she came to the prayer meeting and said, "Guess what? I got the job! I am so happy."

The congregation was so delighted for her. They all prayed and gave thanks.

This pattern of positive prayer and expectation went on, and people began to have goals and tried hard to be positive. They were beginning to learn the message that if they tried,

God would help them the rest of the way. But they also had to remember to quiet their minds and listen for instruction. As a consequence of practicing these activities the church was soon bursting at the seams in terms of attendance. They had lots of new members and plenty of money to fix up the cracks and put on a new roof.

The little church mice were now even warm at night and found more crumbs than they had ever imagined. The church was hosting weddings and many other happy events. There seemed to be all kinds of little crumbs left around. So for the first time in their lives, the little church mice were getting really good food and plenty of it.

They even had enough to share with less fortunate mice. They were indeed so happy that they were the ones who had thought of this plan in the first place. They thanked God and danced around the candle. Pretty soon, some of the coins were spilling off the offering plates, and folks left them there for the janitor who had a sickly wife. Now, even he had enough money to get her the medical help she needed to get well. And, you know what? She *did* get well.

It was all so much fun. Mr. and Mrs. Mouse got new outfits. Mr. Mouse got a new suit, and Mrs. Mouse got a new pink apron and a new pink bonnet without holes. The little Boy Mouse had new rompers, and the Girl Mouse got a new dress. Everybody got new slippers! They were so happy.

They even had enough money left over to buy a big chunk of cheese. This is because the janitor left some of the money for them. They said, "We've learned a lesson in prosperity! We'll never forget it!"

Now, the little white church is one of the most prosperous in the state. It's not only prosperous, but the congregation shares its bounty and remembers to be thankful for it.

And, of course, the little church mice lived happily ever after.

Going to Fairyland

I was feeling extremely bored one long, hot day. I thought I would lie down on my bed and dream that I was in Fairyland. As quick as a wink, and before I knew it, I was in Fairyland!

As I walked into the entrance of Fairyland, I saw a lot of little elves there to greet me. They were dressed in small acorn hats and wore tiny green leaves for skirts. The elves were so nice. They said, "We are here to guide you into Fairyland." They took my hand and led me along.

Near the path, we came across some birds who said, "Come quickly! We will sing you a song." They sat on a little branch, swinging back and forth. They were so nicely brushed, with every feather lying perfectly. They wore little top hats and long black tailcoats. I thought to myself, *very formal*. Their shirts appeared to be so heavily starched that it was hard to move their little heads. There was a golden finch, a red cardinal (my great-grandmother's favorite bird), and a little chickadee (my favorite).

It seems everyone has a favorite bird. I wonder what that is all about. It must have something to do with personalities and how people view life. Anyhow, we know all birds are world travelers, so they probably have some fun stories about humans.

The little birds played the most beautiful songs and chirped away. Then they said, "Come! Before we go too much farther into Fairyland, we will take you to a tea house."

I decided to accept their gracious offer. Then, as we got close, we could see little mushrooms all around the tea house. The elves had to make me small enough to sit down and have tea. It was great fun, having tea with them.

A little later, they said, "We are going to take you to another tea house." To get to the next one, we had to climb up the stem of a flower and onto the leaves.

We were resting on the most beautiful daisy. It had pink all around it. We sat on the daisy, drank tea, and enjoyed the most beautiful picnic of little sandwiches and everything good. There was chocolate cake with white yummy frosting, which we got all over our faces. There were also cucumber sandwiches, tarts, and other delicious items.

We had the most delightful tea party imaginable. I think I gained an inch around the waist. The elves just looked at me and smiled. They seemed happy that I was having such a good time.

The elves said, "As we go along, you will see some of the most beautiful fairies you have ever imagined! There is the Fairy of Hope, the Fairy of Joy and Laughter, the Fairy of Sunshine, and the Fairy of Dreams. You will meet all of these fairies as we visit their castles!"

We finished our tea, hopped down, and walked along a small path. The path was strewn with little flowers and petals. We came to a bridge over a babbling brook. As we were crossing, we looked down to see frogs and tadpoles and goldfish. They all looked up, seeming to say, "Welcome! Welcome! Welcome to Fairyland!"

Everything was so beautiful! Along the path were all kinds of exquisite flowers. There were white daisies with yellow centers and all kinds of tiny blue violets. There were gorgeous red poppies swaying in the breeze and lovely yellow daffodils. The path was glorious, to say the least. It was as if we were winding through an English garden. My great-grandmother would have loved it.

We came to the first castle. It was glistening white—almost snow white. The windows were made of gold. I thought to myself, *What fairy can this be?* The little elves said, "This is the Fairy of Hope!"

We walked up the solid gold steps and knocked with a solid gold hammer. We walked in and were escorted by two little beetles dressed up in orange coats. They took my hand and escorted me up a long flight of stairs and back around to another area with all kinds of hallways and window seats. On the window seats were pink cushions with long gold tassels. They looked very comfortable. I said to myself, *They probably need these seating areas to rest along the way; this place is so big and has so many hallways that one could easily get lost.*

The colored glass windows were open, and the breeze was flowing in. As we approached, there was a beautiful fairy dressed in a white filmy dress that flowed to the floor. She had long golden hair, and it was in pigtails—much to my surprise. Perched on her head was a jeweled crown. She smiled at me and said,

> I am the Fairy of Hope. The lesson I give is to never give up. Always hope. Hang on to your hopes, and believe in yourself. Hang on to your dreams no matter what. Begin when you are a child, continue until you are very old, and never let go of your hopes and dreams. If you get discouraged, just lie down on your bed, and think of me, the Fairy of Hope. Ask me to touch you with my magic wand, and I will give you hope. Without hope, life is not much fun. Always remember that hope is extremely important!

With that, she came down from her throne, walked up to me, and kissed me on the head. She took her little wand, and while chanting, made a blessing for me by scattering gold dust in the air around me. In an instant, she was gone. I almost thought I was dreaming. It was the most beautiful experience of my life. I had met my Fairy of Hope, and the next one I wanted to meet was the Fairy of Joy and Laughter.

We scurried out to the lawn and dashed off to the pathway that went through a beautiful forest. It contained the biggest pine trees I had ever seen. As we journeyed to see the Fairy of Joy and Laughter, we saw all kinds of beautiful animals, including the most beautiful deer I had ever seen! He was a young, cute fawn. He had white spots all over him.

The fawn's beautiful mother was a soft brown, and she had huge brown eyes that were very gentle. She glanced at me as we strolled by. The father deer was in the distance. He had a big rack with eight points. He seemed to be watching over the fawn and the mother. We saw many bunnies and squirrels with long bushy tails and lots of beautiful birds. Happy elves danced around having fun under big brown mushrooms. They were the forest elves.

As we were on the way to see the Fairy of Joy and Laughter, it seemed that the whole forest was singing and laughing. The closer we got to the castle the more singing and laughing! Her castle seemed to have a calm exterior that radiated a pale blue light.

As we entered, the most beautiful angelic creatures met us. They had little wings and little gold crowns. They smiled and looked like miniature fairies as they glided up to us. Two of them were playing harps, and the other two took us up the stairs to meet the blue fairy—the Fairy of Joy and Laughter. She was dressed in a soft blue see-through outfit. She had a beautiful blue crown studded with many glittering diamonds. It sparkled when rays of sun fell on it. In a rather lengthy speech, she said,

> I am the Fairy of Joy and Laughter. My job is to make you laugh and be happy. You have to be happy from the inside. The way to do that, if you are sad, is to go inside and seek

peace in your heart. Say, "I have many things to be happy for," and count your blessing one by one. You will always find something to be happy about. Since I am the Fairy of Joy and Laughter, I like beautiful music, and I like to dance. I like nature and the outdoors, and I like the stars and the moon. The silver crescent moon is my very favorite. This is because it can catch all your tears when you have a problem. You can also sit in it and think pleasant thoughts—always a good way to feel better.

I also love the warm sunshine and the sunbeams and the rainbows after a storm. All of these things are free. We can all enjoy the twinkling stars, the full moon, the silver crescent moon, the sun, the meadows, the rivers, and streams. We can all dream in our silver crescent moon and be thankful for what we have. Being thankful is an important part of being happy!

We can all enjoy the beautiful flowers, the fresh air, our friends, and our families. If we don't have friends and family where we are, we can still enjoy nature because nature is our friend. Nature gives us many things. Remember that the Fairy of Joy and Laughter also stands for thoughtfulness, kindness, thankfulness, and laughter. Remember to be happy and help other people to be happy. My message is to enjoy yourself as you go along your chosen path in life. So, remember to laugh; laughter will bring you great joy and many surprises.

It's good to be thankful for and appreciate what we have, never complaining; we should be thankful for the food we eat, our bodies, our health, and for a higher power to talk to.

Just remember that I am the Fairy of Joy and Laughter. You can always count on me. I am here to remind you to be happy and to count your blessings: your mother and/or father, your school, and your country, America, where you are free. Be thankful for all these things and treat Mom and Dad gently. I am the Fairy of Joy and Laughter!

She then took her magic wand and blessed me, saying, "I grant you great joy; may you always remember to be happy!"

I bowed down to her and made a curtsy, saying, "Thank you, Fairy of Joy and Laughter! I am so happy to meet you!"

With that, the other tiny fairies took my hand and escorted me out of the blue castle. We went on our way to meet the next fairy.

I thought. *My goodness, this Fairyland is so beautiful; I don't know what to expect next.* My friends took my hands, and we came to a beautiful meadow that smelled of clover. There were four-leaf clovers everywhere, which meant good luck!

There were also all kinds of pretty wildflowers (the names of which I do not know) in the meadow. There were little black bumblebees with sheer wings you could see as they sat on flowers. There were honeybees that gathered nectar to make honey. There were huge dragon flies flying around. The sky was bright blue, with not a cloud in sight.

We decided that since the sun was so warm, we would lie down and take a nap. We found a place in the meadow that had soft green turf and fell asleep. The next fairy we were going to meet was the Fairy of Sunshine. We napped for about a half hour under a big daisy so as not to get sunburned. Soon, one of the little elves tugged at me, saying, "Come on, it's time to go to the castle of sunshine."

We walked down a tiny path made from pebbles of different sizes and colors. Flower petals strewn across the path made it easier on our feet as we were walking. We soon came to a bright-yellow shimmering castle. We were greeted at the door by two little drummer men. They looked like crickets and wore big green shoes and red tailcoats. They sported the tallest hats I had ever seen and carried little black canes. Bowing, they said, "We will take you to see the Fairy of Sunshine!"

As we walked down the corridor, we suddenly saw her throne. There she was… the Fairy of Sunshine! Her golden yellow dress flowed to the floor, and she had a brilliant smile and long red hair that wound around her dress. She had a little turned-up nose. How appropriate for the Sunshine Fairy to have freckles. Her crown and wand were solid gold, sprinkled with gold dust.

She smiled as she greeted us and said, "I am the Fairy of Sunshine. I fly around the world and bring sunshine to lonely parents. I warm the earth with sunshine that makes the crops grow."

Hearing these words, I became warm and started to glow. I swear I could see her heart glowing through her gown.

She continued, "When you are lonely, just call for the Sunshine Fairy, and you will feel me like a warm presence all around you. You may say, 'Miss Sunshine, I need some sunshine in my life, and I will be there."

With a small wink of the eye, she vanished. She was on her way to bring sunshine to a lonely child who had just called her. She left the most beautiful ray of sunshine behind her you have ever seen! It was cool and beautiful. But at the same time, it spread deep warmth all around us and felt very pleasant.

In the meantime, the little cricket men came to get us. They said, "Come into the kitchen, and we will warm you with a cup of sunshine."

So we all sat down and were served cups of sunshine that had just been warmed up. We felt so grand and beautiful. I thought to myself, *This Fairyland is really something!*

While we were sitting there, I said, "I had no idea that we had all of these beautiful fairies!"

The elves said, "Just wait until you see the next one. That will be even more surprising to you. I thought to myself, *What more can we expect?*

Then the elves said, "Close your eyes! We are going to fly on a pink carpet to the next place!"

So we closed our eyes, and before I knew it, we were flying on a bright pink carpet. As I opened my eyes, we whizzed right into the most beautiful pink living room you can imagine. The chairs, couch, and pillows were all pink. The carpet was a soft luxurious pink that left footprints when we walked on it. We proceed to the dining room, where the tablecloth was pink and the table was set with pink, gold-trimmed china. At the head of the table was a tiny pink fairy! She said, "Sit and dine with me!"

We were served dinner and pink lemonade. We had pink strawberries and pink ice cream for dessert. Even the hot dish was pink—made with tomatoes. Everything we ate had red or pink in it. The pink lemonade was served in a great big crystal pitcher.

At the end of the table, the pink fairy was dressed in a gorgeous pink dress with huge fluffy sleeves. She had a great big pink bow in her dark brown hair. She was gorgeous, with large brown eyes and long lashes. She said,

> I am the pink fairy. I am the Fairy of Dreams who paints the rainbow. The rainbow stands for luck and inspiration. It is a reminder that when the going gets tough, you need to keep going because the pot of gold is waiting at the end of the journey. Most folks are unaware of the fact that I have hidden small pots of gold along the way for inspiration. If school gets tough, you keep trying. If parents are crabby, you keep going.

The reason I call myself the Fairy of Dreams is that I want to remind you to take leisure time and enjoy things along the way. Enjoy the little things: smiles, friends, holding hands, comforting little brothers or sisters, and helping others. Enjoy each day. Some folks also call me the Fairy of Determination because I am here to give encouragement. There is a saying that determination is one of the most important things you can have in life. You can have all kinds of things—money, good looks, smarts—but not one of these is as important as determination. All successful people have determination. Sprinkle your determination with all the qualities and gifts the other fairies have granted you, and you will indeed have a great life.

With that, she stood up and bade us good-day, and the most beautiful pink color filled the whole room and spread dew like mist over us. It had a fantastic aroma that smelled like roses—pink ones of course!

After meeting with the Fairy of Dreams, we left Fairyland. For the rest of my life, the lessons I learned there came in handy.

The Pink Cloud

I stayed home because I was sick one day. As a matter of fact, I had the flu—terrible stuff—and I was sure I was going to fall behind in my school work. I was lying in my bed with a thermometer, aspirin tablets, and all kinds of blankets. My mother was fussing with me. Finally, she got irritated and said, "You are just acting like a spoiled brat! I'm going to go downstairs and watch some TV. You can just stay here by yourself!"

So I thought to myself, *This is going to be very boring. I think I will imagine something pretty.* Soon, I was relaxed and dreaming. All of a sudden, I became terribly afraid. I soon learned to relax and thought, *God will take care of me. He will put wings on me, and I will be safe.*

So I just decided that I would float. I quickly found myself on the most beautiful pink cloud that seemed to snuggle right up to me and massage my shoulders, my feet, and my legs. It felt so soft on my face and was so comfortable that I decided to just lie there and get well. It reminded me of the cotton candy we ate at the Minnesota State Fair because it sticks to your face. But it was such a friendly, soothing cloud.

After I was there for some time, I indeed felt a lot better. So I tried to stand on the cloud, but that didn't work very well. Then I decided to lie down for fear of putting my foot through the cloud.

I thought, *I wonder where this cloud will take me?* So I peeked over the edge and saw that I was flying over the city. I could see the capital in St. Paul, Minnesota, where I live. I thought, *Oh well, surely the cloud will know how to get me back home.*

We flew among the chimney tops and through the trees and over the Minneapolis-St. Paul International Airport. At one time, I saw that we were right by my friend's house! I could peer inside and see that she was also sick. She was lying in bed under tons of blankets; her favorite teddy bear was tucked in beside her—the one she told me she never slept with. She would never guess how I found out her secret. Wow, it really is so much fun to fly!

A couple of birds flew by and said, "Hi!" and waved at me. They winked at me too! I swear that I recognized one of them. I think he is the red cardinal my mother likes to feed. She is absolutely crazy about birds. He certainly seemed to know who I was.

I then began to think, *This pink cloud must know where my house is.* I was having such a wonderful time flying around. Pretty soon, however, I said out loud, "I wish I was back in my bedroom, surrounded by the heap of blankets my mom piled on me."

I felt a gentle tug, and my mother was bending over me. She said, "I was trying and trying to wake you up! It was as if you had gone somewhere and could not hear me."

I looked up at her, smiled, and thought to myself, *If only you knew where I've been and how much fun I had!*

That's when she took my temperature and found the fever was gone. She looked astonished and said, "That is the quickest recovery I have ever seen. Is there something you're not telling me?"

I said, "Mother, why would you say that?"

"Well, because it is such a remarkable recovery."

Just then, the red cardinal flew by and gave me the *hi* sign and a wink. "I knew I recognized that bird," my mom said. "I swear that bird winked at you, though I surely must be losing my mind."

I just snuggled under the covers and chuckled.

Whenever I get sick, I'm going to wish for that pretty pink cloud and go flying on it. It certainly made me feel better a lot quicker. The only bad part was realizing I would have to go to school the next day.

Timmy

On the way to school one day, I noticed that a group of kids was picking on a little boy named Timmy. Apparently, Timmy was mentally challenged, and the kids liked to taunt him and make fun of him. I thought, *I wonder why these kids are so cruel?* My mother had taught me never to be cruel; consequently, I never taunted people. I thought, *What if I was that person? How would I feel if people treated me like that? My feelings would really be hurt.* How really cruel and unkind they were.

The little boy seemed very sad. Every once in a while I noticed big tears in his eyes. I thought, *Why would anybody want to be so mean? I will make a point of observing this child.* I came to school early one morning when he was early too, so I thought, *I will walk behind him. He won't notice me.*

As I walked close to him, I felt a kind of warm vibration. He seemed to be a really kind child. I thought, *Sometimes kids can be so cruel; they have the nicest clothes and the nicest things, but this little boy doesn't seem to have much of anything. But strangely enough, he seems to have a sweet glow about him. I'm going to keep following him and learning more about him.*

My Aunt Dee Dee taught me that sometimes, if you're very curious and give a person a chance, you'll learn something interesting about that person. You'll discover things about him or her that other people don't take the time to notice. You may even learn a lesson or two.

Keeping him in close view, we walked along a strange new path to school that went through the woods. It was very pretty. *Why hadn't I ever thought of going this way to school?* I wondered. Suddenly, he stopped. He was looking at a small bird that had fallen out of its nest in a tall tree above us.

I saw a bird fall from a tree a couple of summers ago. Some children grabbed it, threw it back and forth, and played with it until it died. I was wondering what this boy would do with the fallen bird.

He gently picked up the little bird. He was so careful with it that the mother bird flew down from her perch and appeared to be totally unafraid of him. She seemed to trust the little boy. She was chirping away a mile a minute and looking up at the boy, as if to say, "Could you help?"

For some odd reason, the little boy seemed to be able to communicate with her. Although he didn't say anything, the little bird was not frightened. So the boy was able to climb up on the fence and put it back into the nest without any problem. The other babies in the nest were not disturbed in the least. It was indeed amazing. I thought, *What a kind boy!*

After he put the little bird back in the nest, the mother bird—small and red-breasted—chirped him the most beautiful song I ever heard. I thought to myself, *What a beautiful experience. I'm glad I'm not one of these cruel kids. They've missed out on one of the loveliest things I have ever seen.*

The little boy seemed to love and understand nature. Indeed, when I followed him to school other times, the birds chirped as he went through the forest, and not one of the animals was afraid of him.

More than the usual number came out; it was as if they wanted to greet him and visit with him.

Now I know why God created mentally challenged children. God needs more love in the world. And for some reason, although these children aren't especially good at reading and writing, they seem to have the gift of great love. They are God's beloved children and have come to teach us about love and kindness and how to protect and care for nature. They are indeed special!

I will always remember Timmy.

God Gives Me Opportunities

God is always near. When you have a serious problem you can't discuss with your teacher, your mom, dad, or your friend, you can tell your troubles to God because he loves you. He also loves for you to talk to him.

He is your best friend. He always has time for you because he adores you. You're very special to him, and you can always have a conversation with him.

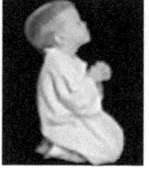

These are song lyrics written especially for this book; make up your own music!

> God gives me opportunities.
> God gives me opportunities.
> I have to listen carefully
> Because he gives me opportunities,
> Opportunities, opportunities,
> Because he loves me.

Delores (Dee) Ray

You must listen carefully.
You must listen carefully
Because God wants to speak to you.
God will give you instructions,
But you must listen carefully,
So he can speak to you.

He talks very softly.
To hear his voice you must be very still,
So you can hear his whisper in your heart.
He surely will nudge you.
He can speak to you with an inner voice,
But you must be quiet and listen carefully.

Be very, very quiet,
and God will talk to you
Because he loves you.

God loves me.
God loves me.
He always has time for me.
He cares if I am hurt.
He is my best friend.
He doesn't care if I'm black or white, rich or poor.

He loves me.
He'll teach me.
He'll answer me because he loves me.
He doesn't care if I'm pretty or smart.
He loves me,
Especially me.

He has a plan for me.
He sent for me, especially me.
Gave me special talents that are unique.
God wants me to be the best I can.
He'll help me
Because he loves me.

Who does he love?
He loves me!
Who?
Me!
Especially me.
I'm special to him.

Opportunity, opportunity,
He'll give me opportunity
Because he loves me.
He'll help me find a way,
But I must listen carefully,
Must listen quietly, so he can talk to me.

Delores (Dee) Ray

It may be a feeling.
It may be a song I hear.
It may be a hunch I get.
But I must learn to be aware,
So he can get in touch with me.
I must trust him.

I must listen carefully to him.
He is always near me.
He always can be found.
He is my best friend,
And he loves me
Who?
Me!

Especially me!

Sarge

Sarge was a wiry Irish terrier puppy, born into an unloving family in the northern woods of Minnesota. The children were not taught to be kind, and they kicked him and pulled his tail. Consequently, he had big sad eyes.

Sarge's fur was all matted, tangled, and dirty, and he was very thin from lack of food. He also had wood ticks stuck in his skin. He looked very scruffy indeed.

It seemed there was just no hope for this forlorn puppy.

Meanwhile...

In a suburb of St. Paul, a lovely lady had lost her husband suddenly and was very lonely. She started wondering if a nice puppy would be a good companion. Everyone was trying to discourage her. They repeatedly told her that puppies are lots of work. You have to train them, feed them, walk them, and so forth. On and on they went with all the reasons she shouldn't get a puppy. "You won't be able to go on vacation either," they said, "because someone else has to care for the puppy if you do."

The lady became very discouraged by this talk. On the other hand, she couldn't get the longing for a puppy of her very own out of her thoughts: *How nice it would be to have a puppy all to myself.*

The puppy would greet her when she woke up in the morning, and it would eat when she ate and sleep when she slept. Furthermore, she could walk with the puppy, play with the puppy, and just plain love the puppy.

She thought more and more about how fun it would be to have a puppy. But how would she get such a puppy—one that would be just right for both her *and* the puppy?

Well, it so happened that the lady, Shirley, had a vacation cabin up north where she sometimes went with her family. One particular fall day, she decided to drive up to the cabin in the woods unusually early, before the rest of her family arrived.

Not a Day Too Soon

As she was driving, she suddenly had a strong feeling that she should go a different way to the cabin. Traveling down a rough gravel road, she was wondering why in the world she chose this route to the cabin. There was one bump after another, and her black car was completely covered in dirt from the dusty road.

Whatever possessed me to drive this awful road? she thought to herself. However, being a cheerful and optimistic person, she decided there had to be a reason for such a strong inner urging to go that way. She decided to look at it as an adventure and see what was in store for her.

Wait! Did that little sign at the side of the road say, "Puppy for Sale?"

She quickly turned her car around. Sure enough, that's what the sign said. It was in front of an old neglected house; the paint was peeling off. The yard was full of clutter. Could there possibly be a puppy living here?

She was soon to find out.

As she approached the screen door to the house, she was greeted by the sad eyes of Sarge. It was as if he was expecting her.

She had never in her wildest dreams thought of an Irish terrier. Maybe a small lapdog, but this was clearly no lap dog. Still, those sad eyes just spoke to her soul. He seemed to be trying to communicate a message to her in his puppy language: "Please take me with you."

Suddenly, a very gruff lady appeared at the door and said, "So what do you want?"

Shirley explained that she had seen the sign by the road. The unfriendly lady said, "This is our last dog; no one seems to want this one. We're selling him at a reduced price."

Shirley thought to herself, *I can see why.* This little Irish terrier was a mess; he was underfed, dirty, and had badly-matted fur. He probably needed his shots too. And on top of that, he may be sick. Still, when he looked at her with those soulful eyes, she heard herself saying, "Yes, I will take him."

She heard the lady say to her husband, "She'll take him, so you won't have to shoot him tomorrow."

I didn't arrive a day too soon! Shirley thought.

Sarge, with grateful eyes, climbed into the seat beside her and put his head in her lap.

They reached the cabin just as the rest of the family arrived. They looked surprised to see Sarge, but he wagged his tail so happily that they immediately fell in love with him.

Shirley realized at that moment that Sarge loved kids. They petted and loved him, and he seemed so pleased with himself.

When Shirley got back home, she took him to the vet. As she suspected, he was a very sick doggy. It turned out that he had Lyme disease, and it would be a long way back to recovery.

They were both up to it. She made him his very own doggy bed, which he loved. He woke her up every morning and was always by her side. They took walks, ate at the same time, watched TV, and generally had fun times together. When Shirley suddenly got very sick, he stayed right by her side, in his loyal and affectionate way, and helped her recover.

The last time I saw Sarge, he had the happiest eyes I have ever seen on a dog!

The Green Frog

This is the story of the Green Frog—a *very* green frog! It was a Friday night, and I was tired of watching TV. I didn't like the program Mom and Dad were watching.

I decided to go outside and play. Usually at night, I'm not allowed to go very far from home, but I felt adventurous for some reason. So I walked across the street, through the field, and down a small hill not far from the house.

I had a friend there called Green Frog. I would go down and talk to Green Frog and watch him sitting on his green lily pad—his head cocked one way or the other. He always seemed to sense when I was lonely.

When Mom and Dad were busy and I had no one to play with, I would often go down and talk to the frog. Although he never answered me, he seemed to listen to me and know what I was thinking.

Froggy Thoughts

On that particular evening, it was still fairly bright but getting close to dusk. I decided to take the trip down to see my friend—Green Frog—because I was especially lonely.

As I looked at him sitting on a rock in the pond, he beckoned me to come and sit on his back. I thought he was being a silly frog. How could I sit on his back? I thought I was way too big and I might squish him. His thoughts seemed to say, *Hurry up; come on. Come and sit on my back.* He glanced up at me and blinked his eyes. So I thought I'd try it and hoped I wouldn't hurt my new friend.

Stepping cautiously as I went to sit on Green Frog, I grew small enough to fit perfectly on his back. I grabbed hold of him around his neck. He whispered to me, "Hang on, and I will take you for an exciting little adventure."

At first, he was very cautious, hopping from lily pad to lily pad. Some of the lily pads had beautiful white flowers on them, like pretty lilies. We hopped from lily pad to lily pad, and the fragrance was wonderful. It was so much fun and exciting. He was very careful, so I didn't get my toes wet in the water.

We hopped all over the creek and visited some of his friends. We visited fine dragonflies flying by with their wings turning into the wind. They seemed very friendly to the frog. We saw some other little bugs on the lily pad that were his friends.

As we hopped along, we saw tadpoles and baby frogs. They asked his advice. "When do we get to be big frogs?" It was interesting to see how many water friends he had. We visited the swamp, floated down the creek, and had a grand old time together.

Fireflies and Fairies

There seemed to be a party going on in one part of the creek. Fireflies were there, and they were all lit up and flew around so that everyone could see. They made a little bonfire and rubbed little lanterns together to make a fire out of the weeds.

There were some grasshoppers too, rubbing their legs together to make music. Crickets sang their songs, and frogs croaked their tunes. What a lively orchestra! Some little fairies came out and danced among the lily pads.

The fairies were especially beautiful. They had lovely wings of gold and silver. Their dresses were very filmy; some were orange, some were blue, and others were purple. They danced and had a marvelous time. They seemed to simply float along the lily pads.

A dance line began to form with all these magical, friendly, happy creatures. It was just so beautiful and peaceful. It seemed like we stayed out all night. What a marvelous time!

All of a sudden, I looked at my watch and thought, *Mom and Dad will be done watching TV by now and might be sleeping on the couch (they often fell asleep watching TV). I should leave the party now and get back before they wake up.*

The frog said he would deliver me to the edge of the creek. Then all the forest animals and insects said good-bye to me. They added, "Come another day during the daytime. We have a secret spot where we can have a tea party."

I said goodbye to all of them and hopped onto the frog's back. We flew over the edge of the creek, and I hopped off. I shook his hand and said, "Goodbye. I'll see you tomorrow."

I walked up the grassy hill and across the dark street. Mom and Dad were fast asleep, and the TV was still blaring. They'd be surprised if they knew of my adventure. I turned off the TV and left them sleeping there. I crawled into my snuggly little bed and had pleasant dreams.

The Magic Gown

This is a story about what happened many years ago in the month of June. It was a sunny afternoon in Shoreview, Minnesota, a suburb of St. Paul. Everyone was gone. Grandpa had gone to Montana to see his mother, who was eighty-six years old. My father was fishing, and I was waiting for my friends to come over and take me to breakfast.

They had called me at 8:30 a.m. that morning, but it was now ten o'clock. I was beginning to feel lonely, so I slipped into my imaginary magic gown. My magic gown is something I use when I'm lonely or when I want to go into my fantasy world and visit my fantasy friends.

It was a beautiful day for a fantasy, so I slipped into the gown. It was sheer—with all the colors of the rainbow—and it fit over my clothes. It had a big sash around the waist, a Peter Pan collar, and really fluffy sleeves. I had rainbow slippers to match made out of delicate satin.

I walked out on the deck, down the steps, and out to the yard. The grass was covered with sprinkles of water from a light morning shower.

I sat under a beautiful Russian olive tree. I love Russian olive trees because they become a very different color when the sun shines on them—a silvery blue. I sat there for a while and contemplated the day, the afternoon, and what might happen.

As I was sitting there, up popped a little fairy elf. He sat on a mushroom and began a conversation with me. He was very funny and made me laugh. He flipped his wings around and did somersaults. He was really quite delightful.

All of a sudden, we got another little shower, and he quickly folded his wings up over his head to stay dry. I thought this was very clever. So I put the hood of my rainbow magic gown up, and I didn't get wet either.

We looked around and saw the rain falling around us. In the distance, we could see a robin tugging at a worm that had come out of the earth during the rain. The robin had a bright red breast, and he was very happy.

How Elves Travel

The fairy elf told me a story about how he traveled to other planets, as well as to far-flung places on earth.

"Well," I asked, "how do you travel when you go to other planets?"

He answered, "When I want to go around and see elves and fairies from other planets, I hop on a beam of light, close my eyes, and I'm there in an instant!"

Oh my goodness! I thought. *That would be so much fun—hopping on a beam of light to travel anywhere you wanted to go in the universe!*

He told me about visiting the moon and stars and how the stars twinkle. He was such a delightful little elf!

Pretty soon, he called some of the other fairy elves to play ring-around-the rosy and hopscotch. They formed a chorus line and waved their little wings. It was *so* great! They entertained me for over an hour. Then I heard my friends coming for breakfast, so I quickly scurried into the house.

Pancakes and Milkshakes

My elf friends disappeared instantly. I could swear I saw a small beam of light, and they just jumped on it, waved good-bye, and said, "We'll see you tonight!"

I quickly took off my magic gown because I wanted to keep my adventure a secret. I also knew I couldn't tell anyone about my elf friends. So I quickly threw the gown in my dresser drawer with a smile and waited to leave for breakfast. Pancakes and a chocolate milkshake—that's what I thought I'd have.

My friends arrived and said, "Come on, we have to hurry. We're late."

One reached up and brushed my hair. She said, "There appeared to be a beam of light in your hair, but the minute I touched it, it disappeared."

Jack said, "Oh, girls are so silly."

I just smiled, thinking about my little friends and the fact that they'd return this evening.

My elf friends later told me about the little beam of light they had left on my hair. They explained how they travel around on beams of light, going from house to house, making other little children happy when they're lonely.

It's really nice to have an elf friend. Maybe you'll find one too!

Thunder: Megan's Friend

This story is for Megan—a story of thunder. Megan was a four-year-old Irish girl who was very darling. But she was always afraid of thunder, so she thought, *I'm never going to get over being afraid of thunder. I have to find out what thunder is.*

One particular night, she knew there was going to be a terrible thunderstorm. It was going to rain and splash on her bedroom window. She would have to be brave and stay awake, so she could really find out what thunder was.

Megan hopped into her warm flannel pajamas, jumped into her bed, and snuggled under the oversized quilts her grandmother had made. There were so *many* of them, with different plaid squares and fun-colored yarn holding them together.

Indeed, this was a very cozy bed. She lay down on her soft pillow with the embroidered pillowcase. It was her favorite pillow, given to her by Erin, her mom.

Her pretty mother had always provided the best bed for Megan. In fact, it was a waterbed, which she had gotten for Christmas.

I'm going to stay under this big quilt, Megan thought, *where I'll snuggle and stay awake in this thunderstorm no matter what happens. I'm going to see what this thunder business is all about.*

A Ride on a Raindrop

Sure enough, she had been in bed for only about half an hour when the thunderstorm came. The thunder rolled, the lightning cracked, and her window blew open. She heard something whisper, "Megan, Megan. Do you still want to find out what thunder is? Come to the windowsill! Come to the windowsill! Get on a raindrop, and I will fly you to the thunder! I will fly you to the thunder!"

She said, "I can't! I'm deathly afraid of thunder. I don't want to meet thunder!"

The whisper said, "Don't worry! Don't worry! I will protect you. Get on the raindrop. Get on the raindrop!"

How silly. How can I do that? she thought. *But if I'm ever going to learn about thunder, I'd better follow the instructions.*

So she sat on a big raindrop on the windowsill. Before she knew it, she was up in the air, meeting Mr. Thunder, who was blowing and puffing.

"Hi, Megan," Mr. Thunder said. "I understand you were worried about thunder and wondering who I am. I'm not *so* bad. I just make a lot of noise. We *have* to have thunder and lightning in order to have rain. Come with me, and I'll show you!"

So Megan climbed on Mr. Thunder's back and hung on to his long hair. Before she knew it, Mr. Thunder was traveling to the farm country. He said, "Without thunder, we would not have rain. Without rain, we would not have crops, and without crops, we would not have food to eat. So we have very good thunder—very good thunder!"

Megan looked down, and, sure enough, there were some wheat plants growing and some corn stalks coming up. They would supply food for people and animals.

Mr. Thunder's Brother

Megan was flying high above the farmland. Mr. Thunder was making good thunder with all of the rain to make the crops grow. "See, I am very, very good thunder," he said. "But of course, I have a bad brother, who is Mr. Bad Thunder. But if you surround yourself in white light and ask for protection, you will never have to worry about Bad Thunder. I will show you what Bad Thunder does. Hang on! Hang on!"

Megan and Mr. Thunder whizzed over the forest and the neighboring town, and there was Bad Thunder! Bad Thunder had just used his power the wrong way. He had instructed the lightning to strike down a little tree, and he had hurt the tree. Bad Thunder had even made a bolt of lightning strike a cow. There really *was* a Bad Thunder, but most of the time, thunder is good.

Mr. Thunder said, "See, I want you to know that there's good thunder and there's bad thunder, just like there are good people and bad people. Most of the time, the thunder is good, so don't be afraid. I am Mr. Good Thunder, and you will see me most of the time. We will always try to protect you from Bad Thunder."

Megan smiled at that. *My*, she thought, *this Mr. Thunder is so nice!*

Mr. Thunder said, "Come now, I'll take you back to your home. Then you have to slide off and get back into bed. Your mother will never believe you've been flying around up here on Mr. Thunder!"

So that's what he did. He took Megan back to the raindrop, and she stepped on it and splashed onto the windowsill. She hopped right into bed just in time for her mother, Aaron, to come in and say, "Megan, I know you're afraid of thunder."

Megan just looked at her mom, smiled, and said, "Me? Afraid of thunder? Of course not, Mother. What gave you that idea?" Her mother looked totally surprised.

She went over to tuck Megan in bed, and as she stroked her long brown hair, she said, "Your hair is damp, almost as if you've been flying through the rain with Mr. Thunder."

She kissed her and winked as she closed the door to her bedroom. With that, Megan fell fast asleep and was never afraid of thunder again. She now realized that most of the time, thunder was her friend. From then on, when there was rain or a storm, she snuggled up in her warm bed and enjoyed the raindrops splashing on her window.

Sometimes she'd hop out of bed, open the window, and wave at Mr. Thunder. She often thought of Mr. Thunder—now her friend—and waited for him to come and visit her.

Pleasant dreams!

Grandmother's Remedy

I once had a very serious problem, and I didn't know why or what to do about it. It was one of those days when your mind just thinks, thinks, thinks, and everybody is upset with you. You have problems, *and* you don't know what to do with yourself. Your mind races, *and* you are nervous. Your mother yells at you, *and* you're in trouble at school. You flunk your math class, unci your best girlfriend flirts with your boyfriend. You have just broken your new radio, *and* you don't have a thing to wear to a party at school. It just seems that the whole world is falling down around you in little chips, and you're just sitting in the middle of them, slowly being covered up by more and more chips! You can hardly even breathe!

So I was thinking, thinking, and thinking. What can I do? I can't even think straight. And then I remembered what my grandmother had once told me to do. I thought, *Well, I don't have anything to lose. I've thought and I've thought, and I have tried everything, so I think I'll try her technique."*

I got up, went to my room, and shut the door. We had no locks, or I would have locked it too. I got up on my bed and hoped no one would come in.

Deep Breaths, Marshmallows, and the Pink Balloon

I began to take deep breaths—in through my nose and out through my mouth—just as Grandmother had instructed. I continued doing that: in and out, in and out, in and out. I kept breathing slowly in, slowly out until I began to calm down and relax.

Then I took a *really* big, deep breath and held it until I counted to five. Then I let it out. I did this five times: breathe, hold (one, two, three, four, five), and out. I also listened to my breath as it went in and out slowly.

I pretended I was a marshmallow. My feet turned to marshmallows. My legs turned to marshmallows. My shoulders, head, and tummy turned to marshmallows. I was just a huge marshmallow—a spongy marshmallow. My whole body was a marshmallow, jumping around and feeling very soft and flexible. I was a marshmallow person.

I felt so relaxed and wonderful. I thought, *This is kind of fun! I don't even have to worry about my problems any longer. Who cares? I'm having a good time!*

I remembered Grandmother said that if you want to make wishes or you want to get away, you must pretend you are in a pink, clear, flexible balloon. It's so clear that you can see through it, like the soap bubbles I blow. It's soft as a cloud to lie on. She said to make a balloon, and then hop up into the balloon and pretend you're inside it. Then, lay your head and feet on a pink pillow.

Once you have created this clear pink balloon and are inside it, let it go out of the house and up into the clouds. There, you can relax and do anything you want. You can stay up there until it grows dark. Then you can see the stars and the moon twinkling. You just stay up there and relax, focusing your mind on anything you want. There's even a little TV screen to put there if you want to. You can ask for help from anybody and put your problems up there. It's like a computer. You can say, "Let the problem be solved." Then, you just go on doing your thing, and the answer will come to you. If it doesn't come to you right away, it will come to you later.

You just have to put all your problems up in the universe. The universe then gives you helpful insights and ideas. While you're there, nothing can reach you—not even problems. Just relax and enjoy yourself.

You can go anywhere. You can go to England to see castles. You can go to Africa and see beautiful animals. You can go to your grandma's house. You can go to the lake, or you can go to the farm. You can just stay up there and turn your TV screen on, and let it solve your problems by giving you insights. Or you can just float among the stars.

One particular day, I decided to relax on this fluffy cloud. I thought of all my problems, and then I put them in the computer and thought, *That will take care of it. I'll get the answers when I return. I'm not going to think about them any longer.*

I stayed on the cloud, relaxed, and had fun. I knew I could return home anytime I wished. I was perfectly safe, so I went to visit the stars. They twinkled so brightly!

There are many mysteries in the stars. One mystery is about a lion, and one is about beautiful maidens. Another one is about the "man" in the moon. There are all kinds of fantasies and stories up there.

I figured that if I floated long enough, I might come upon another galaxy where other people lived. But I wasn't brave enough to do that. So I just went around our city and flew over the houses of a couple of my friends. I had a wonderful time.

All of a sudden, I got the message that I should go back because my mother might want me home for dinner. So, *hop*, and there I was—back at home. Just then, my mother knocked on the door and said that dinner was ready.

When I came out, I was really happy and smiling. My mother said, "My, you look so pretty. What have you been doing today? You look like you are in a very pleasant mood. In fact, I think we should take you to a movie tonight!"

I was very pleased and said to myself, *Thank you, Grandmother. That really helped, and I had a wonderful time.*

The ABC Story

This is my ABC story. Once upon a time, there was a little girl named Amanda who wanted to learn the ABCs, so her mother offered to help her. "In your mind's eye, it will help if you think of the following pictures and how they fit in your life."

So Amanda began the game of learning the alphabet.

A is for apple—a big, red, juicy apple. I can eat the apple. My name starts with an A! So, A is for apple.

Then there's the B. What does B stand for? B is for boy. Daddy is a boy. I love my daddy! He's nice! So, B is for Boy.

Amanda was really catching on.

C is for cat. I have a big fluffy cat, with a tail that goes swish, swish, swish. He has big yellow eyes and long whiskers. When I get really close to him, his whiskers tickle me, and I laugh. So, C is for cat.

D is for Aunt Dee Dee, who works in an office in the cities. Once in a while, she comes to see me. D is for Dee Dee.

E is for eat. I like to eat my mother's and grandmother's cooking. I like their chocolate chip cookies. My favorite candy is black jellybeans. I also like to eat oatmeal. (I'm just *kidding.*) Bubble gum is fun also. E is for eat.

F is for fat. I have an aunt who's kind of fat. My aunt is a good cook. Other things are fat too. I have a fat dog. My dog's name is Brandy, and he's fat. My mom put him on a diet! F is for fat.

G is for good. I am a good girl. My mother reads me bedtime stories when I'm very good. I'm a good girl, *most* of the time. G is for good.

H is for happy. When I get to ride in the car and go to Disney World, I'm happy! When I go to school, I'm happy. When I see my mother and dad, I'm happy. When I watch cartoons, I'm happy. H is for happy.

I is what you see with. I have two eyes, although eyes is not spelled with an I. Eye is spelled with an e. My, this alphabet is confusing! I is for eye?

J is for June. I have an Aunt June. My Aunt June lives with my Uncle Bob. They are nice people. I get to see June often because she lives in my hometown. My aunt was born in the month of June and is named after that month. Isn't that fun? J is for my Aunt June and for the month of June.

K is for kite. My dad helps me fly a kite. It's fun. It blows and blows in the breeze. K is for kite.

L is for love. My mother loves my dad, and that's why I'm here! L is for love. My family is filled with love. I love my grandmother, I love my cousins, and I love my family. L is for love.

M is for my mother. My mother loves me. My mother cooks for me. My mother does this, and my mother does that. My mother does everything. M is for mother.

N is for naughty. Sometimes I'm naughty. One day, I spilled the dog's water on purpose. That was naughty. One day, I splashed in the mud puddles and got my new shoes all wet. That was naughty. One day, I spilled my soup when I didn't like it. N is for naughty. Sometimes *I'm* naughty!

O is for open. Open the jar. Open the door. Open the can. Open the bottle. Open, open, open! O is for open.

P is for Paul. I have an Uncle Paul. He plays the accordion, and he sings children's songs. P is for Paul.

Q is for quiet. When I go to sleep, my mother says, "Be quiet. Be very, very quiet because the stars are out. They are listening to see if you are quiet." When you want to go to sleep, you have to be very, very quiet. Q is for quiet.

R is for run. I love to run. I love to run and skip rope. I love to run and hop. All of us run! My dog runs. My cat does not run. I run, and my mother runs after me. R is for run.

S is for sit. Sit down, Amanda; sit down, and be a good girl. Sit, sit, I say that, and my dog sits! Sit, Brandy, sit. S is for sit.

T is for two. I have two eyes. I have two ears. I have two feet, and I have two hands. T is for two.

U is for up! Up goes the hot air balloon that we are riding in. U is for up!

V is for victory. That's when Mother tries to convince Dad to do something he doesn't want to do. My mother has many Vs! V is for victory.

W is for work. My mother works as a nurse. My dad owns his own hardware store and a video store. Mother works. Dad works. I work. I help Mother clean the house. I help Dad at the store. W is for work.

X is for kisses. XXX means kiss, kiss, kiss! Kiss my mother. Kiss my dad. Kiss my doggy. Kiss my grandmother. Kiss is on Valentine's cards also. X is for kiss.

Y is for you. I'm me and you are you. You go to the store. You ride in the car. You have friends. You are my friend. You is for you.

Z is for zipper. Zip my coat; zip my jacket. Zip up my jacket to go out and play. Z is for zipper.

ABCDEFGHIJKLMNOPQRSTUVWXYZ!

My mother helped me learn the alphabet!

The Sad Dog

This is a story about a real dog with long floppy ears with little curls on the ends and big sad eyes. He's white and has irregular brown spots. This dog's name is Rusty. He's a sad little dog because he can't find the big white bone he buried last spring.

Rusty had been away all winter out in the country hiding in a barn to keep warm. He decided he was very much in need of his bone, so he went out to look for it. But no matter where he looked, he couldn't find it. He looked everywhere, and he was getting hungrier and hungrier. He wanted to find that bone and chew on it. He thought the bone would give him a warm, fuzzy feeling because he had no family and no friends.

The more he looked, the more depressed he became. He was going along, minding his own business, when a mean little boy threw sticks and stones at him. *My,* he thought, *that little boy is really a brat.* In fact, the boy was the monster of the neighborhood.

The lonely little dog yelped and yelped as he ran away. He hid under the bushes, so the little boy couldn't see him. *I didn't know human beings could be so bad,* he thought.

The little dog was really sad and lonely. *Doesn't anyone ever love a homely little dog with irregular spots?* he wondered and wished someone would love him.

Some Good Advice

Rusty got so upset that he sat up on his haunches, looked up into the sky, and said, "I think I'll talk to God, because God can help me." So he said to God, "I'm a sad, lonely little puppy dog, and I'd like you to help me. Would you please consider this?"

All of a sudden, a voice flashed into his mind. God said, "Little puppy, God loves you, but you need to think more positively. You need to think things through on your own." Then he instructed, "Go deep into the forest and meditate; go deep within yourself. You will find the answer, and you will also find out where your bone is."

The little puppy decided to do just that. He tramped over leaves and fallen trees and thick underbrush until he was deep into the darkest part of the forest. He then came upon a narrow little path that led him to a cool blue pond.

He looked in the pond and saw a reflection of himself. He seemed quite happy then. He said, "Hey, I'm not half-bad-looking when I'm happy. My eyes are kind, and they twinkle. My ears are really kind of cute and curly, and I kind of *like* my irregular spots. Maybe I'm not such an ugly doggie after all. If God loves me, how can I be such a bad dog?" He decided to sit there and contemplate and meditate.

The little doggie contemplated and meditated for a long while, but he just couldn't seem to find an answer. Then he decided, "Oh well, I'll just relax for a minute."

The minute he relaxed, his mind seemed to get a flash that he'd hidden the delicious bone behind someone's garage the day the owners were away from home.

He thought, *That's where I hid it! I hid it in a fancy neighborhood, behind a huge brick garage when no one was home. I think I'll dash over there right now and see if it's there.*

He stepped onto the narrow path and then walked under a big pine tree. The pine tree was wet with rain, and when he brushed against the branches, it sprinkled him with water. It certainly was refreshing after that long walk through the forest.

He walked over to a blackberry patch where a little bluebird was picking at the berries. He looked at Ms. Bluebird, smiled, and said, "Good afternoon!"

Ms. Bluebird said, "Chirp, chirp! Good afternoon to you too."

Then Rusty chased a little blue butterfly that said, "Come on, come on! Let's have a run!" It was a pretty, bright blue butterfly. *Boy,* Rusty thought, *this is really a neat butterfly.* It was almost as if the beautiful blue butterfly was leading him out of the dense woods.

On his way out of the forest, Rusty stopped to speak with a little black-and-white skunk. He saw some squirrels that were having a party. They said, "Come and play! Come and play!

He said, "Oh no. I have to go and get my bone, but I'll come back and play another day!"

He thought, *This is a friendly forest. A doggie could make a lot of friends here. I'll never have to be lonely again. I'll just come to this forest with all these friendly animals!* He was feeling very happy and content by then.

Just as he was leaving the forest, he approached the edge of a meadow. There, he saw the *most beautiful deer he had ever seen. It had a huge rack of horns.* He thought, *Oh my! This is a beautiful, magnificent deer. I'm going to have to be strong like that in my thinking: proud and upright!*

He walked over to the big deer and felt very tiny beside him. The father deer just looked down at him and nodded his head. "Good morning! I like you, little dog!"

The little dog wagged his tail and was so happy. He said, "Goodbye! I'll be back!"

The Fancy Neighborhood

Rusty dashed out of the forest edge, across the meadow, down the sidewalk, past the grocery store, the butcher shop, the sweet shop, and the fancy dress shop. He continued around the corner, up the hill, through the traffic light, and into the fancy neighborhood.

"Whew—my goodness! There's someone home now. I hope I can get my bone. I'll remember to be courageous like the deer. I'll also remember that God said to follow my intuition." Rusty stood there for a minute and thought, *I'll go around the back way and stay in the shadows. They'll never even see me.*

So he went around to the back, staying in the shadows. He dug up his bone near the edge of the garage. By gosh, he was surprised it was still there! He proudly carried it away. Just as he walked under the streetlight, out from the other side of the house came another little male dog.

This little dog said, "Hi! I live in this house. Who are you, and where do you live?"

Rusty answered, "I live in a poor neighborhood. I just fend for myself. I don't belong anywhere."

The little male dog said, "I see you found your bone."

"How did you know it was there?" Rusty asked.

The little male dog answered, "I was very lonely one day, so I dug a hole and came across your bone. But I covered it up again because I thought surely the doggie that owned it would come back for it someday. I haven't seen any dogs in this neighborhood, and I don't have any doggie friends. So I've been waiting a long while for you to arrive."

Rusty was so astonished that he dropped his bone. He said, "You've been lonely?"

"Yes, I live in this big expensive house, and I have my own dog house and fresh meat to eat every day and all the bones I want. But I'm still very lonely because I don't have any fun. I don't know how to romp in the forest. I don't know how to run down the alley. I don't know how to have fun"

Rusty looked at him and said, "That is really sad, but I can teach you!"

"Could you? That would be wonderful—absolutely wonderful! When can we start?"

"We can start right now. But first, I have to eat this bone because I am very hungry."

The little dog said, "I have plenty of food. I've been too sad and lonely to eat, but now I feel happy. We can eat this nice steak that my master cut up for me. We can rest for an hour, and then we can go on an adventure. Perhaps we can go exploring around midnight."

"That would be great," Rusty said. He went with his new friend to his doghouse and couldn't believe what he saw—a big dish of steak!

The little male dog cautioned him, "Don't eat too much; if you do, you won't feel good."

Rusty restrained himself. He ate only a bite of the steak and found fresh water. After he drank some water, he and his new friend were going to go to sleep, but they talked for a while.

They took a half-hour nap, and pretty soon, it was midnight. They decided to scamper off. It was the perfect match because one had plenty of the good things, and one had a sense of adventure.

A Night on the Town

So they ventured out into the night. They saw people who get wild and unruly at night in the bars, dancing girls, and people going out to dinner. Rusty showed his friend the city and its nightlife. They also heard the sound of buses and horns that honk at night.

They had a grand time. The male dog was so impressed with Rusty. He knew all of this neat stuff and how to fend for himself.

Rusty said, "Tomorrow, I'll take you for a walk in the forest. Now I have to go. I have to find a park bench to sleep under."

The little dog said, "Oh no! You can come into my doghouse and sleep."

"What will your master think?" Rusty asked.

"I think he'll be happy that I found a doggie friend because he *does* love me."

So the two little doggies went back and slept in the cozy doghouse.

The next morning, the lady of the house came out. She could not believe her eyes! There were two doggies, and they looked almost alike. She called to her husband and said, "Look here, look here! Our Blackie has found another doggie friend. They look almost alike, except that Blackie has black spots, and this doggie has rust-colored spots." She knew his name *had* to be Rusty.

She could tell by looking at Blackie that he wanted Rusty to stay. She said, "I can see that Rusty is an adventuresome doggie. I'm sure he'll take care of our Blackie. I never wanted Blackie to go out by himself before, but now that he has a friend to be with, it will be okay. When he goes out with Rusty, Rusty will protect him. I feel sure of it."

They knew they could make a beautiful home for both Blackie and Rusty. "They'll have the best of both worlds because one knows the street life, and one knows the good life. Together, they'll be able to learn from each other. They'll be perfect together."

The doggies looked at each other, wagged their tails, and lived happily ever after.

The Mouse's Tea Party

As I was walking through the woods one day, I found something lying on the ground. It was like a little mouse but seemed to be too tiny, and its eyes weren't open yet.

I thought, *Oh dear! I wonder where he fell from.* I really didn't like mice, so I took off my shoe and put him in my sock. I carried him and wondered to myself, *What am I going to do with him? I probably should take him back to his mother.*

I looked around and looked around. Sure enough, there—under some bushes—was a cozy little mouse nest.

Mother Mouse appeared there and scolded me severely. I said, "Look, it wasn't my fault!" Then I delivered him to her and felt very relieved.

The Mice and the Maypole

As I continued my walk through the woods, I suddenly saw some other mice. They were all dressed up, wearing little pink aprons and straw hats with long blue ribbons streaming from the back. They were all sitting around a beautiful pink mushroom having a tea party!

As they saw me approach, they looked at me and said, "We saw that you just saved our cousin, Baby Mouse, and returned him to his mother. Don't mind his mom; she's a rather ungrateful mouse, but she does have her good points. For instance, she makes the best blueberry muffins you've ever eaten."

Then they said, "Thank you so much. We'd been looking for Baby Mouse all morning but couldn't find him. We're so relieved you found him. Also, we know you're a friend of the green frog in the creek. Why don't you come and join us for tea? We know you're a friend. Even though you're a human being, we feel you're a safe one."

Momma Mouse touched me with her magic wand, and I became small enough to sit on a tiny silver mushroom. We sat around a pink mushroom having our tea, drinking out of little pink cups. We all had a great time. The mice told stories and had fun laughing, and playing Ring Around the Rosy.

It was close to May Day, and they all ran around the maypole, throwing little violets and May flowers up in the air. They had little May baskets that they gave to each other and even gave one to me. They were having the best time.

I thought to myself, *This is the best tea party I've ever been to. These mice are so friendly! I'll never be afraid of mice after this.*

I told them I had to go because I had to get to the other end of the great forest and through the meadow to see my Grandma Dee Dee. They said, "Okay, we'd better make you big again."

I thanked them very much and ran off through the forest and across the green meadow to my grandma's cabin.

Grandmas, Tadpoles, and Secrets

I arrived there just in time for her to say, "I think we're going to go fishing and then go swimming in the creek down over the hill. Get your swimsuit, and let's go!"

I thought to myself, *Should I tell her about the mice?* Then I thought, *Well, my grandma knows a lot, and who else would understand about the mice?* So I told her about my experience.

Then she told me some stories about what *she* had found. She said she used to have a tadpole friend. The tadpole would take her under the water—way under the water—and go swimming and splashing around with the other tadpoles. She said she could never tell her mother either, but she was glad that I had decided to tell her because she'd always had this secret and never had anyone to share it with.

She said, "You know, you should not go by a person's age. Sometimes, people are old when they are young and young when they are old! You just never know whom you can tell secrets to. But you can always tell *me* your secrets."

We laughed and thought, *We can have the best secrets because the older you get sometimes, the younger you get.* We had a great time, fishing and telling each other our stories. She told me to be sure to invite her the next time I went to have tea with the mice.

I said, "I certainly *will* do that!"

A Trip To The Cabin

This is a story about an experience I had going to my Grandma's cabin. Sometimes when I go to her house, we get in the car and take off to the country. She has a big black car and is kind of a fast driver. Once in a while, she scares me a little with her driving, I always have to remind her to fasten her seat belt.

The cabin is in Wisconsin, and the highway patrol likes to give Minnesota drivers tickets. She gets one when I am with her this time. We are chatting away, and she isn't paying attention to how fast she is going. She whips out her Visa card to pay the fine, and we go on our merry way.

On these trips to the country, we drive and drive. It seems like it takes forever. So to make it seem more fun, Grandma stops at the bakery, and we get some wonderful rolls to eat in the car. She also gets a cup of steaming hot coffee. Sometimes we stop for breakfast at a tourist spot. We usually get bacon, eggs, and more black coffee. I can have whatever I want, as long as it isn't pop!

We eat and hit the road again, driving though the beautiful countryside on tree-lined roads from which we see plenty of ponds, rivers, and lakes. Halfway there, we stop for an ice cream cone. Then Grandma wonders why she puts weight on when she goes to the cabin!

Just before we get to the cabin, we come to a really small town where they make cheese. We stop there and get three kinds of cheese, and I get some string cheese.

When we finally arrive at the cabin, we have great fun. My great-grandmother is there. She is old and quite wrinkled. I recognize her right away, even though I have not seen her before. She is very friendly, and we become extremely good pals.

We fish at a lake near the cabin. We catch northern pike, sunfish, bass, and sometimes bullheads. Bullheads are the ones that sting you and are very hard to get off the line. Sometimes James (my godfather), my dad, and my dad's girlfriend come. We have lunch and eat the sunfish we catch after rolling them in corn meal and flying them in hot grease. They are delicious and very good for you.

After dinner we have strawberry shortcakes made from homemade biscuits and fresh picked strawberries, we then watch movies on the DVD player and tell ghost stories.

We have a really good time. We swim and splash and float on our rafts in the water. We go to the sandy beach and play in the sand. We found sand castles!

It is really fun at the cabin in the summer time, the air is fresh and you sleep much better. Sometimes we go out at night with the telescope and look at the stars. They are much brighter up there as they don't have a lot of city lights and pollution. The people who live by my Grandma's cabin are very much environmentalists, and they take good care not to pollute and to keep things healthy for the animals.

When it is real dark and clear, it seems like there are a million stars twinkling overhead. They seem to say "Nicole, wish upon a star, make a great wish."

I said to myself, I will have to make a wish on the next clear night. There is a saying "Wish Upon a Star" I will ask my Grandma Dee Dee about it, she knows about these things. Maybe I can wish upon a star and get a great wish. So I wrote that in my memory bank in my mind and said, "Some time when it is quiet and we are alone, I will ask her if she has wished upon a star and received an answer to her wish."

www.ingramcontent.com/pod-product-compliance
Lightning Source LLC
Chambersburg PA
CBHW060403080526
44583CB00012B/445